JUST

MW00575927

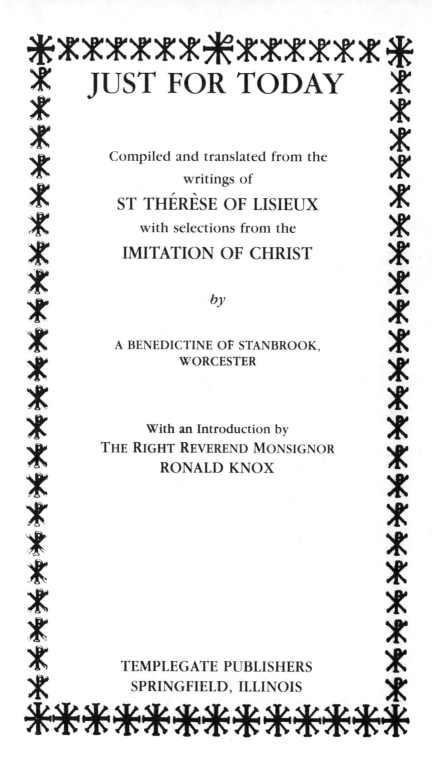

JUST FOR TODAY

Compiled and translated from the
writings of
ST THÉRÈSE OF LISIEUX
with selections from the
IMITATION OF CHRIST

by

A BENEDICTINE OF STANBROOK,
WORCESTER

With an Introduction by
THE RIGHT REVEREND MONSIGNOR
RONALD KNOX

TEMPLEGATE PUBLISHERS
SPRINGFIELD, ILLINOIS

© Burns & Oates Ltd.

First published in 1943
Second printing 1949
Third printing 1950
Fourth printing 1953
Fifth printing 1983
Sixth printing 1988

All rights reserved, including the
right of reproduction in whole or in
part, in any form.

ISBN 0-87243-121-5

Templegate Publishers
302 East Adams St./P.O. Box 5152
Springfield, Illinois 62705

LIST OF ABBREVIATIONS

Bk...ch... = IMITATION OF CHRIST.

     C. = CONSEILS ET SOUVENIRS.

     E. = ESPRIT DE SAINTE THÉRÈSE.

     H. = HISTOIRE D'UNE AME : La Bienheureuse Thérèse de l'Enfant Jésus. *Published in* 1923.

     L. = LETTERS.

  N.V. = NOVISSIMA VERBA.

     P. = POEMS.

   Pr. = PRAYERS.

 Sum. = SUMMARIUM.

INTRODUCTION

THE compiler of this anthology has been happily inspired to sit between two treasure-chests, dealing out to us a jewel first from this, then from that, like matched pearls. One is the *Imitation of Christ;* the other, the writings of St Teresa of Lisieux. Just five centuries divide them in date. Your first impression, when you see the pearls so well matched, is to exclaim at the resemblance; your second, that after all Christian piety does not alter with the ages, and there are certain rock-bottom truths which need constant reassertion, rather because our wills are so weak than because our memory has let the tradition slide. And indeed, the *Imitation* was a favourite book with Sœur Thérèse, as it has been with so many ardent natures.

The author of the *Imitation* was a voice crying in the wilderness; a voice so well content to be anonymous that scholars can still wrangle over his identity. He warns us that we are not to care who said this, but to pay attention to the thing said. The case is otherwise at Lisieux; there, the personality of the Saint, the very lineaments of her features, are the public property of mankind; it is her message that is in danger of being forgotten. Put a card of the Little Flower in your copy of the *Imitation*, and it will cease to be anonymous; she did not write it, but, much more importantly, she lived it.

Our minds tend to confuse what is simple with what is easy. Look up what day you will in this accusing calendar, and you will find something which is so simple that you could have thought of it for yourself; so far from easy, that you have spent a lifetime not doing it. It is a very Newgate Calendar of our infidelities. Out of the mouth of two witnesses every word shall stand; and here are two witnesses, faithful as those of the Apocalypse, to brush away our feeble excuses with their pitiless realism. Let the phrases be copy-book phrases, if you will; they have been traced in laborious copper-plate, by a fifteenth-century ascetic, and retraced, God knows how laboriously, by a childish hand, contemporary with ourselves.

Day to day utters speech, and night to night shows forth knowledge. This is a book to keep by your bedside, so that you can turn to it before you make your examination of conscience, and read in it the diary of what you have left undone. May it reveal the thoughts of many hearts, and rekindle in them the love of Jesus Christ.

R. A. KNOX.

JUST FOR TODAY

Let not the authority of the writer offend thee, whether he was of little or great learning; but let the love of pure truth lead thee to read. If thou wilt receive profit, read with humility, simplicity and faith.

Bk. I, ch. v.[1]

O Lord, who hast said: Unless ye become as little children ye shall not enter the Kingdom of Heaven: grant us, we beseech Thee, so to follow, in humility and simplicity of heart, the footsteps of the Virgin, St Teresa, that we may secure everlasting rewards. Amen.

Collect of the Mass of St Teresa.

JANUARY 2

Christ will come to thee, discovering to thee His consolation, if thou wilt prepare Him a fit dwelling within thee. Many a visit doth He make to the internal man, sweet is His communication with him, delightful His consolation, much peace, and a familiarity exceedingly to be admired.

Bk. II, ch. i.

She had been looking at a picture in which Our Lord was represented with two children. The younger child was sitting on His knee caressing Him, whilst the other shyly and reverently kissed His hand. "I am the little one on Our Lord's knee,' she said,, "who looks up fear-

[1]Challoner's translation.

I

lessly and kisses Him. I prefer him to the other child, who is behaving like a grown-up person."

E.

JANUARY 3

What shall I give Thee for so many thousands of favours? O that I could serve Thee all the days of my life! O that I were able, if it were but for one day, to serve Thee worthily !

Bk. III, ch. x.

> Oh! what is my life but a passing hour,
> So brief I can scarce call it mine!
> Then just for to-day I will love Thee, Lord,
> That each moment of it may be Thine!

P.

JANUARY 4

In this, most of all, hast Thou shown me the sweetness of Thy love, that when I had no being Thou hast made me; and when I strayed far from Thee, Thou hast brought me back again, that I might serve Thee; and Thou hast commanded me to love Thee. O Fountain of everlasting love, what shall I say to Thee? How can I ever forget Thee, who hast vouchsafed to remember me, even after that I was corrupted and was lost? Thou hast beyond all hope shown mercy to Thy servant, and beyond all my desert bestowed Thy grace and friend-ship on me.

What return shall I make to Thee for this favour? for it is a favour not granted to all, to forsake all things and renounce the world, and choose a monastic life. Can it be much to serve Thee, whom the whole creation is bound to serve? It ought not to seem much to me to serve Thee; but this seems rather great and wonderful to me, that Thou vouchsafest to receive one so wretched and unworthy into Thy service, and to associate him to Thy beloved servants.

Bk. III, ch. x.

Opening the Gospels my eyes fell upon these words: *Going up into a mountain he called to him whom he would* (Mark iii, 13). These words sum up the mystery of my vocation and of my whole life, and above all the mystery of the special graces bestowed on my soul. He does not choose those who are worthy, but those whom He is pleased to call. As St Paul says, quoting Exodus: *I will have mercy on whom I will have mercy* (Exod. xxxiii, 19). *So then it is not of him that willeth, nor of him that runneth, but of God that showeth mercy* (Rom. ix, 16).

H.

JANUARY 5

Love feels no burthen, values no labours, would willingly do more than it can; complains not of impossibility, because it conceives that it may and can do all things. It is able, therefore, to do anything, and it performs and effects many things, where he that loves not, faints and lies down.

Bk. III, ch. v.

For the first time in my life I was to pay a visit without my sisters, and the visit was to be to a bishop! I, who never spoke unless someone asked me a question, had now to explain my reasons for wanting to enter Carmel, and show that my vocation was genuine. What it cost me to overcome my shyness! But how true it is that: *love complains not of impossibility, because it conceives that it may and can do all things.*

Nothing but love of Our Lord could have made me face these difficulties and those that were to follow, for I was to pay dearly for my happiness. Looking back today, the cost seems trifling, and if it had still to be paid I would willingly go through trials a thousand times worse.

H.

JANUARY 6

To some I speak things common, to others things more particular; to some I sweetly appear in signs and figures, to other in great light I reveal mysteries.

Bk. III, ch. xliii.

Since Christmas Céline had begun to share my most intimate thoughts. Our Lord wished us to make progress together, and so united us in a bond closer than mere ties of blood by making our very souls sisters. I love to recall our conversations at that time, as we sat in the belvedere looking out at the starry sky. I believe that we received many graces; as the author of the *Imitation* says: *To some I sweetly appear in signs and figures, to others in great light I reveal mysteries.* He revealed Himself to our hearts, and the veil that hid Him was almost transparent. To doubt would have been impossible; whilst yet on earth we had found, through love, Him whom we sought, so that faith and hope were in abeyance.

H.

JANUARY 7

Many love Jesus as long as they meet with no adversity; many praise Him and bless Him as long as they receive consolations from Him. But if Jesus hide Himself, and leave them for a little while, they either fall into complaints or excessive dejection.

But they that love Jesus for Jesus' sake, and not for any comfort of their own, bless Him no less in tribulation and anguish of heart, than in the greatest consolation.

Bk. II, ch. xi.

Life is indeed, as you say, hard and wearisome; when Jesus hides Himself it is difficult to begin the day's work. What has become of our Friend? Does He not see our burden and anguish of heart? Where is He, and why does He not come to comfort us?

Do not fear, Céline. He is there beside us. Like a beggar He asks for this grief, these tears, that He may apply them to souls, to our own soul, and He will repay us magnificently. He feels having to hurt us, but He knows that it is the only way to teach us how to know Him as He knows Himself and to become gods. How great is our soul's destiny! Let us remain above this earth and passing things; in those regions we breathe a purer air. If Jesus hides, we guess His presence!

L.

JANUARY 8

Love often knows no measure, but is inflamed above measure.

Bk. III, ch. v.

When I come to die and see God, who will pour out His love upon me for all eternity when I can no longer prove mine by making sacrifices, I should not be able to endure it if I had not done on earth all in my power to please Him.

E.

JANUARY 9

How can he be puffed up with the vain talk of men, whose heart in truth is subjected to God? All the world will not move him whom truth hath established in humility.

Neither will he be moved with the tongues of all that praise him, who hath settled his whole hope in God. For, behold, they also that speak are all nothing, for they shall pass away with the sound of their words: but *the truth of the Lord remaineth for ever* (Ps. cxvi, 2).

Bk. III, ch. xiv.

When still a novice she heard two members of the Community, one after the other and independently, express their opinion of her. One judgement was the exact opposite of the other, yet both were given with equal good faith and conviction. "Since then," she said, "I have paid no attention to the opinions of others, and this attitude of mind has become habitual, so that praise or blame make no impression on me whatever."

H.

JANUARY 10

(Christ.) As I willingly offered Myself to God, My Father, for thy sins, with My hands stretched out upon the cross, and My body naked, so that nothing remained in Me which was not turned into a sacrifice to appease the divine wrath; even so must thou willingly offer thyself to Me daily in the Mass, for a pure and holy oblation, together with all thy powers and affections, as heartily as thou art able.

Bk. IV, ch. viii.

In the year 1895 I was given the grace to realize more than ever how much Our Lord wishes to be loved. I was thinking of souls who willingly offer themselves up to divine justice, drawing down punishment upon themselves so that the guilty may be spared. I saw how noble and generous this action was, but felt no inclination to imitate them.

From the depths of my soul I cried: Oh! my divine Master! is Thy justice alone to receive victims of holocaust? What of Thy merciful love? On every side it is ignored and rejected . . . souls destined to receive its bounty turn instead towards creatures, seeking for one instant to enjoy their worthless affection, instead of throwing themselves into Thy arms and the fiery furnace of everlasting love. Oh! my God! is Thy rejected love to remain locked up in Thy heart? If souls could be found to offer themselves as victims to Thy merciful love, it seems to me that Thou wouldst quickly consume them in its flames.

H.

JANUARY 11

This is a favour to Thy friend, that he should suffer and be afflicted in this world for the love of Thee, how often soever, and by whomsoever Thou permittest it to fall upon him. Without Thy counsel and providence, and without cause, nothing is done upon earth.

It is good for me, O Lord, that Thou hast humbled me, that I may learn Thy justification, and that I may cast away from me all pride of heart and presumption. It is advantageous for me that shame has covered my face, that I may rather seek my comfort from Thee than from men. I have learned hereby to fear Thy impenetrable judgements, who afflictest the just with the wicked, but not without equity and justice.

Bk. III, ch. 1.

January 10 was, as I have described to you, the day of
our dear Father's triumph. This feast can be likened to
Our Lord's entry into Jerusalem on Palm Sunday. Just
as his divine Master's triumph was to be followed by
the bitter Passion, so was his own short-lived glory to
be changed into suffering. Our Lady's heart was pierced
by the Passion of her Son, as ours are by the humiliation
and suffering of the one we love best upon earth.

H.

JANUARY 12

Take it not to heart when thou art forsaken by a
friend; knowing that one time or other we must all part.

Bk. II, ch. ix.

About that time I chose two little girls of my own
age as friends, but, alas, how fickle are human hearts!
One of them returned home and was away for several
months; I did not forget her and welcomed her back
lovingly, only to receive a casual glance. I was deeply
hurt, and resolved not to play the part of a beggar for
so inconstant an affection.

However, God has endowed me with a faithful heart,
which once given is never taken back, so that I still love
my school-fellow and pray for her.

H.

JANUARY 13

O that with Thy presence Thou wouldst inflame,
burn, and transform me into Thyself, that I may be
made one spirit with Thee, by the grace of internal
union and by the melting of ardent love!

Bk. IV, ch. xvi.

Now all enkindled is my heart,
  On fire with love's consuming flame
That to its inmost core does dart,
  Till fire and fuel seem the same,
United, never more to part.

P.

JANUARY 14

Nature labours for her own interest, and thinks what gain she may reap from others: But grace considers not what may be advantageous and profitable to herself, but rather what may be profitable to many.

Bk. III, ch. liv.

She had heard how much trouble a poor Sister suffering from neurasthenia was giving the infirmarians:

"How I wish I had been infirmarian," she cried, "and had her as my patient! Grace would have spoken louder than nature, for I feel an attraction for such work. I would have put so much love into my nursing, that I am sure I would have made her happy, remembering that Our Lord said: '*I was sick and ye visited me*'." (Matt. xxv, 36.)

N.V.

JANUARY 15

Oh! how humbly and lowly ought I to think of myself: how little ought I to esteem whatever good I may seem to have. Oh! how low ought I to cast myself down under the bottomless depths of Thy judgements, O Lord: where I find myself to be nothing else than nothing!

Where, then, can there be any reason for glorying in myself? where, any confidence in any conceit of my

own virtue? All vainglory is swallowed up in the depth
of Thy judgements over me.

Bk. III, ch. xiv.

How good God is to have given wings to my soul and
lifted it up! I am not afraid of the hunter's net, for *a
net is spread in vain before the eyes of them that have
wings* (Prov. i, 17). It may be that later on this present
time will seem to fall short in many ways, but nothing
surprises me any longer, and I do not grieve at the sight
of my weakness. On the contrary, I glory in it, and expect to go on finding fresh imperfections in myself. The
light to see my own nothingness is more help to me
than understanding the mysteries of faith.

H.

JANUARY 16

(Christ.) Thou oughtest to seek the grace of devotion
earnestly, to ask for it fervently, to wait for it patiently
and confidently, to receive it thankfully, to keep it
humbly, to work with it diligently, and to commit to
God the time and manner of this heavenly visitation,
until it shall please Him to come unto thee.

Thou oughtest chiefly to humble thyself when thou
feelest inwardly little or no devotion: and yet not to
be too much dejected, not to grieve inordinately. God
often giveth in one short moment what He hath a long
time denied. He giveth sometimes in the end, that
which in the beginning of prayer He deferred to grant.

Bk. IV, ch. xv.

I am indeed far from being a saint; the dispositions
I am in prove that. Instead of rejoicing in my aridity,
I ought to attribute it to my lack of fervour and fidelity,

I ought to grieve at the way I go to sleep at my prayer
and during my thanksgiving, and yet, I do not grieve.
Instead, I cannot help thinking that little children please
their parents as much when they are asleep as when they
are awake, that surgeons put their patients to sleep for
an operation, in short, that the Lord *knowest our frame.
He remembereth that we are dust* (Ps. cii).

H.

JANUARY 17

Seldom do we find anyone so spiritual as to be strip-
ped of all things. For who shall be able to find the man
that is truly poor in spirit, and divested of all affection
for created things? His value is as of things that are
brought from *far and from the uttermost coasts* (Prov.
xxxi, 10).

Bk. II, ch. xi.

If thou lookest to thyself, thou canst do nothing of
this of thyself. But if thou confidest in the Lord,
strength will be given thee from heaven, and the world
and the flesh shall be made subject to thee.

Bk. II, ch. xii.

In order to love Jesus, to be His loving victim, the
more weak and wretched we are, the more easily can
His transforming and consuming love work in us.
Merely to wish to be a victim is enough, provided that
we are willing to remain poor and without strength of
our own, and therein lies the difficulty, for, as the
author of the *Imitation* says: *Who shall be able to find the
man that is truly poor in spirit?* He does not tell us to
seek him amongst great souls, but *afar,* that is, in low-
liness and abjection.

Oh! let us remain *far away* from all that glitters, let
us love our littleness, love our inability to feel what is
going on in our soul; then we shall be truly poor in
spirit, and Jesus will fetch us from *afar* and enkindle
within us the fire of His love.

L.

JANUARY 18

What does solicitude about future accidents bring
thee, but only sorrow upon sorrow? *Sufficient for the
day is the evil thereof* (Matt. vi, 34). It is a vain and unprofitable thing to conceive either grief or joy for future
things, which perhaps will never happen.

Bk. III. ch. xxx.

> I do not lift my eyes to see
> 　　The clouds next day may bring;
> From stain of sin, Lord, keep me free
> 　　This day, beneath Thy wing!
>
> I can endure just for today
> 　　The cross that Thou wilt send;
> The daily grace, for which I pray,
> 　　Will help me to the end.

P.

JANUARY 19

Many are found to desire contemplation; but they
care not to practise those things which are required
thereunto.

Bk. III, ch. xxxi.

Marie, no doubt thinking that I was quite pious
enough for my age, would only allow me time for my
vocal prayers, and none for mental prayer, much as I
would have loved it. One of my mistresses at the

Abbey asked me how I spent my whole holidays, when I remained at home. I answered shyly that by drawing the curtains of my bed I could make a little recess in which I could hide, and there I would sit and *think*. "Oh!" said the good nun, laughing, "and pray what do you think about?" "About God, the shortness of life, eternity; in fact, I just *think*."

My mistress remembered this, and later used to remind me of my *thinking* and asked if I still kept it up. I realize now that I was really praying, whilst my divine Master gently taught my soul.

H.

JANUARY 20

If we would use but a little violence upon ourselves in the beginning, we might afterwards do all things with ease and joy. It is hard to leave off our old customs, and harder to go against our own will. But if thou dost not overcome things that are small and light, when wilt thou overcome greater difficulties?

Resist thy inclination in the beginning, and break off the evil habit; lest perhaps by little and little the difficulty increase upon thee. Oh! if thou wert sensible how much peace thou shouldst procure to thyself!

Bk. I, ch. xi.

I will have thee learn the perfect renunciation of thyself, according to My will, without contradiction and complaint.

Bk. III, ch. lvi.

At the first sound of the bell she would lay down her work, or break off a conversation, however interesting. If she were sewing at the time, she would leave the needle in the unfinished stitch. Whilst the bell was ringing, her sister Marie continued writing something she had just told her, and that she herself was afraid of forgetting. The Saint reproved her gently but firmly: "It would be better to lose that and obey the Rule. If you only knew what you are missing!"

Sum.

JANUARY 21

Search not curiously to know what shall befall thee, but rather study to inquire what is the will of God, well pleasing and perfect.

Bk. I, ch. xxv.

This is what thou shouldst wish, that in life or death, God may be always glorified in thee.

Bk. III, ch. xlix.

Thou hast taught me, O God, from my youth: and till now I will declare Thy wonderful works, unto old age and grey hairs (Ps. lxx, 17).

What will old age be in my case? I see no reason why it should not be now, rather than later: two thousand years are no more in the sight of God than twenty years—or even a single day.

Do not think that I want to leave you, as though it were a greater privilege to die young; I only wish to please Our Lord. As He seems to be calling me out of this life, I cannot help rejoicing; for God has no need of anyone, least of all myself, to do good on earth.

H.

JANUARY 22

If thou hadst the purity of an angel, and the sanctity of St John the Baptist, thou wouldst not be worthy to receive or handle this sacrament. Take heed to thyself, and see what kind of ministry has been delivered to thee by the imposition of the bishop's hands.

Bk. IV, ch. v.

The privilege of handling the consecrated vessels, and preparing the linen cloths which were to come in contact with Jesus Christ was a great joy to me. I realized how fervent this ought to make me, and often recalled these words spoken to a holy deacon: *Be ye clean, you that carry the vessels of the Lord* (Is. lii, 11).

H.

JANUARY 23

To Thee I lift up mine eyes; in Thee, O my God, the Father of Mercies, I put my trust. Bless and sanctify my soul with Thy heavenly blessing, that it may be made Thy holy habitation, and the seat of Thy eternal glory; and let nothing be found in the temple of Thy dignity that may offend the eyes of Thy majesty.

Bk. III, ch. lix.

> Make of my soul a sanctuary,
>   Thy holy dwelling-place;
> Make it a garden of delight
> Where every flower seeks the Light:
>   The glory of Thy face.

P.

JANUARY 24

What great matter it is, if thou, who art but dust and a mere nothing, submit thyself for God's sake to men, when I, the Almighty and the Most High, who created all things out of nothing, have, for thy sake, humbly subjected Myself to man?

Bk. III, ch. xiii.

I will humble myself and subject my will to that of my Sisters in all things, without waiting to consider whether they have the right to give me orders or not. No one, my Beloved, could claim this right over Thee, and yet Thou didst obey not only Our Lady and St Joseph, but even Thy executioners.

H.

JANUARY 25

Let Thy name be praised, not mine, let Thy work be extolled, not mine; let Thy holy name be blessed; but to me let nothing be attributed of the praises of men.

Thou art my glory; Thou art the joy of my heart. In Thee will I glory and rejoice all the day; *but for myself I will glory in nothing but in my infirmities* (II Cor. xii, 5).

Bk. III, ch. xl.

Someone had said to her: "You are a Saint!"

"No, I am not a saint, nor have my deeds ever been those of a saint. I am a very little soul whom God has overwhelmed with graces. In Heaven you will see that I am speaking the truth."

N.V.

JANUARY 26

For Thy will and the love of Thy honour ought to be regarded above all, and to comfort and please a man more than any benefits whatsoever, which he hath received, or can receive.

Bk. III, ch. xxii.

There is a verse of the Psalms which I recite very reluctantly every day at Sext: *Inclinavi cor meum ad*

faciendas justificationes tuas in aeternum, propter retri-
butionem (Ps. cxviii). (I have inclined my heart to do thy
justifications for ever, for the reward.) I then hasten to
add in my heart: Dear Lord, Thou knowest that I do
not serve Thee for the sake of a reward, but simply
because I love Thee, and in order to save souls.

H.

JANUARY 27

O Jesus, the brightness of eternal glory; the comfort
of a soul in its pilgrimage! My tongue cannot express
the sentiments of my heart, but my silence itself speaks
to Thee.

Bk. III, ch. xxi.

Apart from the Divine Office, which, although unworthy, I have the happiness of reciting, I do not look
for beautiful prayers in books; there are so many that
they make my head ache. Besides, it is so difficult to
choose between them, as each is more beautiful than
the other, so that I do like little children who cannot
read: I tell my Heavenly Father what I have to say,
and He always understands.

It seems to me that prayer is just the raising of one's
heart and an upward glance to Heaven, a cry of love
and gratitude in the midst of trials just as much as in
joy. It is the being lifted on to a higher, supernatural
plane, where the soul is enlarged and united to God.

H.

JANUARY 28

What means this most loving condescension, and so
friendly an invitation? How shall I dare to approach,
who am conscious to myself of no good on which I can
presume?

The angels and archangels stand with a reverential awe; the saints and the just are afraid; and Thou sayest *Come ye all to me*! Unless Thou, O Lord, didst say it, who could believe it to be true? And unless Thou didst command it, who would dare attempt to approach?

Bk. IV, ch. i.

Jesus calls; what an invitation! We were an object of horror to ourselves, and Jesus calls us that He may look upon us . . . He comes, and with Him the other two divine Persons of the Blessed Trinity, to take possession of our soul. He made this promise so lovingly when He said: *If anyone love me, he will keep my word, and my Father will love him, and we will come to him, and will make our abode with him* (John xiv, 23). The only condition laid down, the only proof of our love that He requires of us is that we keep His word. Surely this Word can be none other than Himself, for He is the uncreated Word of God.

L.

JANUARY 29

This is that truth by which all vainglory is put to flight. If heavenly grace and true charity come in, there shall be no envy or narrowness of heart, nor shall self-love keep its hold. For divine charity overcomes all, and dilates all the powers of the soul.

Bk. III, ch. ix.

When in the Old Law God commanded His people to love their neighbour as themselves, He had not yet come down upon earth, and considering how strong self-love is, He could not have asked more. But when Christ gave His new commandment to the Apostles,

He required them not merely to love their neighbour as themselves, but as He loved him, unto the end.

O Jesus! I know that Thou canst not command anything impossible; Thou knowest my weakness and imperfection better than I do, and that I could never succeed in loving my Sisters as Thou hast done, unless Thou, my divine Saviour, dost continue to love them in me. In giving this *new* commandment, Thou didst intend to grant me this grace, and it is dear to me because I have the assurance that Thou wilt Thyself love in me those whom I am bidden to love.

H.

JANUARY 30

Be thou, therefore, ready prepared to fight if thou desirest to gain the victory. Without fighting, thou canst not obtain the crown of patience.

Bk. III, ch. xix.

I am eager for these pin-pricks, that wound the heart and make it suffer so intensely. No suffering can be too great if we would win the palm of victory.

L.

JANUARY 31

How can a life be loved that hath so great bitterness, that is subject to so many calamities and miseries? How can it be called life, since it begets so many deaths and plagues?

Bk. III, ch. xx.

We must therefore have patience, and wait for the mercy of God till iniquity pass away, and this mortality be swallowed up by immortal life.

Bk. I, ch. xxii.

It grieved me to see her so ill, and I often said: "How sad life is!" but she would at once correct me: "Life is not sad, but joyful. If you said: How sad is our exile! I could understand; it is a mistake to call what will pass away *life*. We should only apply that beautiful word to what will never die, to heavenly things; and as we already enjoy a foretaste of them upon earth, life is not sad but cheerful and very bright."

C.

February 1

Nature desires to be taken notice of, and to do such things as may procure praise and admiration. Grace teaches us to restrain the senses, to avoid vain complacency and ostentation, humbly to hide those things which are worthy of praise and admiration, and from everything, and in every knowledge, to seek the fruit of spiritual profit, and the praise and honour of God.

Bk. III, ch. liv.

When my divine Master bade me give to whomsoever asks of me, and not ask that what has been taken be restored to me, it seems to me that He was speaking of spiritual as well as earthly possessions. Neither are my own property: I have renounced the latter by my vow of poverty, and the former are only lent to me by God, who is at liberty to withdraw them without my having any right to complain. One's own deep and original reflections, living flames that spring from the mind and heart, are a personal treasure to be jealously guarded. For instance, if I share with some Sister a light I have received in prayer, and she passes this on as her own, I feel that she has robbed me. In the same way, if at recreation a witty remark is appropriated by another and repeated before the Community, the original owner of the saying feels that she has been defrauded of what is hers, and though she does not claim it at the time, yet she takes good care that the authorship becomes known.

But I have been given the grace to be as detached from the treasures of my mind and heart as I am from those of this world. If I happen to think or say anything that pleases my Sisters, I take it as a matter of course if they appropriate it: the thought came from the Holy Ghost, for St Paul assures us that without His inspiration we cannot even call God our Father (Rom. viii, 15). He is at liberty to communicate through me a good thought to another soul, and I cannot consider it as mine.

H.

FEBRUARY 2

The saints and friends of Christ served the Lord in hunger and thirst; in cold and nakedness; in labour and weariness; in watchings and fastings; in prayers and holy meditations; in persecutions and many reproaches.

Bk. I, ch. viii.

A priest had said in a letter to her that Our Lady had not experienced physical suffering.

"Looking at Our Lady this evening, I realized that this was not true. She suffered in body as well as in soul. She suffered from the fatigue of her journeys, from cold and heat, from hunger and weariness. She often fasted. She knows only too well what it is to suffer."

N.V.

FEBRUARY 3

Nature covets to know secrets and to hear news; but
grace cares not for the hearing of news and curious
things, because all this springs from the old corruption,
since nothing is new or lasting upon earth. She teaches
therefore to restrain the senses.

Bk. III, ch. liv.

One day she gave me a striking proof of her interior
mortification. I had received a very interesting letter,
which had been read at recreation in her absence. That
evening she asked if she might read it, so I gave it to
her. When she returned it, I asked her opinion on a
subject which must have given her much pleasure, but
she appeared embarrassed, and then admitted:

"Our Lord asked this sacrifice from me because of the
undue eagerness I showed the other day, and so I did
not read it."

C.

FEBRUARY 4

Without charity the outward work profiteth nothing:
but whatever is done out of charity, be it never so little
and contemptible, all becomes fruitful.

Bk. I, ch. xv.

She often referred to a game which had delighted her
as a child. It was a kaleidoscope, a kind of miniature
telescope through which one saw many-coloured
designs that took on new forms as one turned the
instrument.

"I was filled with admiration, and wondered what
could cause such a marvel, until one day I discovered
that it was simply odds and ends of paper and coloured

wool. Continuing my researches I found three mirrors inside the tube, which solved the problem. This became for me the symbol of a great mystery. As long as all our actions, however insignificant, remain within the sphere of charity, the Blessed Trinity, symbolized by the three converging mirrors, sheds upon them a marvellous beauty and radiance. Our Lord, looking on us through the lens, that is Himself, sees our actions as well pleasing to Him. But if we withdrew from the centre of charity, what would He see? Odds and ends of straw . . . unclean and worthless."

C.

FEBRUARY 5

O how wise was that holy soul that said: *My mind is strongly settled and grounded upon Christ* (St Agatha)!

Bk. III, ch. xlv.

I no longer feel the need of denying myself the solace of affection, because my heart is firmly established in God. Now that my whole heart is His, it has become enlarged, and I am able to love those dear to me with a love incomparably greater than if it had sprung from a selfish, sterile affection.

H.

FEBRUARY 6

O Lord God, my holy lover, when Thou shalt come into my heart, all that is within me will be filled with joy. Thou art my hope and my refuge in the day of my tribulation. But because I am as yet weak in love and imperfect in virtue, therefore do I stand in need of being strengthened and comforted by Thee. For this reason visit me often, and instruct me in Thy holy discipline.

Free me from evil passions, and heal my mind of all
disorderly affections: that being healed and well purified
in my interior, I may become fit to love, courageous to
suffer and constant to persevere.

Bk. III, ch. v.

You are making a great mistake if you think of me as
advancing bravely along the path of self-sacrifice. Every
day I learn by experience how weak I am, but Our Lord
has taught me how to *glory in my infirmities* (II Cor. xi).
I have asked Him to give you also this great grace which
brings true peace to the soul. One turns away from the
sight of one's own wretchedness to look only at Jesus
Christ.

You ask me what are the means for attaining perfection, but I only know of one: Love. Our hearts having
been made for love, let us then love. I sometimes try to
find a better word than *love*, but in this land of exile *the
word that has a beginning and an end* is quite inadequate
to express a spiritual experience, and so one has to be
content with the one word: Love.

But to whom shall we give the love of our hearts, who
is worthy of such a treasure? Is there any human being
capable of appreciating it, and giving us some return?
Only Our Lord can do this, and He gives in return
infinitely more than we can ever give Him.

L.

FEBRUARY 7

From the hour of My birth till My expiring on the
cross, I was never without suffering.

Bk. III, ch. xviii.

Our Lord has always spoilt me. It is true that I have
never been without the cross since I was in my cradle,

but He has given me the grace to love the cross with
my whole heart.

L.

FEBRUARY 8

Endeavour to be patient in supporting the defects and
infirmities of others, of what kind soever; because thou
also hast many things which others must bear withal.
If all were perfect, what then should we have to suffer
from others for God's sake?

Bk. I, ch. xvi.

Let me love Thee more than myself, and myself only
for Thee, and all others in Thee, who truly love Thee, as
the law of love commands, which shines forth from
Thee.

Love is swift, sincere, pious, pleasant, and delightful;
strong, patient, faithful, prudent, long-suffering, courageous, and never seeking itself.

Bk. III, ch. v.

*Greater love than this no man hath, that a man lay
down his life for his friends* (John xv, 13). Meditating on
these words, I realized how imperfect was my love for
my Sisters; I saw that I did not love as Jesus loves them.
I understand now that true charity consists in bearing
with all the defects of our neighbour, in not being
surprised at her weakness, in being edified by the least
of her virtues. Above all, charity must not remain
hidden in the heart, because *no man lighteth a candle,
and putteth it in a hidden place, nor under a bushel; but
upon a candlestick, that they that are in the house may see
the light* (Luke xi, 13). I think this candle must represent charity, which ought to enlighten and cheer not
only those I love most, but *all that are in the house.*

H.

FEBRUARY 9

If indeed there had been anything better and more beneficial to man's salvation than suffering, Christ certainly would have shown it by word and example. For He manifestly exhorts both His disciples that followed Him, and all that desire to follow Him, to bear the cross, saying: *If any man will come after me, let him deny himself, and take up his cross daily and follow me* (Luke ix, 23).

So that when we have read and searched all, let this be the final conclusion, that *through many tribulations we must enter into the kingdom of God* (Acts xiv, 21).

Bk. II, ch. xii.

On this earth where all things change, there is one thing that does not change, and that is the way the King of kings treats His friends. Ever since the standard of the Cross was lifted up, all must strive for victory beneath its shadow. As Theophane Venard reminds us: *The life of a missionary is made up of crosses. True happiness lies in suffering, and if we wish to live, we must first die.*

My dear brother, be glad that the beginning of your apostolate is marked with the cross. Suffering and persecution bring about the reign of Christ in souls more effectually than eloquent preaching.

L.

FEBRUARY 10

O my beloved Spouse, Christ Jesus, most pure Lover, Lord of the whole creation; who will give me the wings of true liberty, to fly and repose in Thee? Oh, when shall it be fully granted me to attend at leisure, and see how sweet Thou art, O Lord, my God?

Bk. III. ch. xxi.

Oh! that I might wing my way
   To Him, who stands upon the shore
Where breaks the dawn of endless day,
   And life's dark shadows are no more!
There shall I find a Mother's smile,
   A Mother's kiss to welcome me;
Safe in the haven of her arms
   My weary spirit fain would be.

P.

FEBRUARY 11

Man's merits are not to be estimated by his having many visions or consolations, nor by his knowledge of Scriptures, nor by his being placed in a more elevated station; but by his being grounded in true humility, and replenished with divine charity; by his seeking always, purely and entirely, the honour of God; by his esteeming himself as nothing, and sincerely despising himself; and being better pleased to be despised and humbled by others, than to be the object of their esteem.

Bk. III, ch. vii.

No sudden splendour broke the grey
   And even tenor of your days,
No ecstasy made you forget
   Your poverty in its bright rays.

Mary, the lowliest can tread
   With confidence the path you trod,
Your life the bright and shining star
   That leads the wayfarer to God.

P.

FEBRUARY 12

O just Father, holy and always to be praised, the hour is come for Thy servant to be tried. O Father, worthy of all love, it is fitting that Thy servant should at this hour suffer something for Thee.

O Father always to be honoured, the hour is come that Thou foresawest from all eternity: that Thy servant for a short time should be oppressed without, but always live within to Thee; that he should be a little slighted and humbled, and should fail in the sight of men; that he should be severely afflicted with sufferings and diseases, that so he may rise again with Thee in the dawning of a new light, and be glorified in heaven.

Bk. III, ch. i.

When we are together in Heaven, we shall love to recall the dark days of our exile. I think the three years of Father's martyrdom were the best and most profitable of our whole life, and I would not exchange them for the most glorious ecstasies. When I think of this marvellous treasure, I am filled with gratitude and repeat the words of the Psalmist: *We have rejoiced for the days in which thou hast humbled us: for the years in which we have seen evils* (Ps. lxxxix, 15).

H.

FEBRUARY 13

Woe to them that disdain to humble themselves willingly with the little children; for the low gate of the heavenly kingdom will not suffer them to enter therein.

Bk. III, ch. lviii.

All my life I have remained a little child. My only occupation has been to please Our Lord by gathering flowers of love and self-sacrifice to give Him.

E.

FEBRUARY 14

Vanity of vanities, and all is vanity, besides loving God and serving Him alone. This is the highest wisdom: by despising the world to tend to heavenly kingdoms.

Bk. I, ch. i.

Many of the young and wealthy people I met at these house-parties are now dead. I sometimes remember their fine country houses and beautiful grounds, and think how useless all their possessions are to them now. *Vanity of vanities and all is vanity, besides loving God and serving Him alone.* Perhaps Our Lord wished me to see the world before my First Communion, so that I might choose freely before I bound myself to Him.

H.

FEBRUARY 15

Son, if thou placest thy peace in any person for the sake of thy contentment in his company, thou shalt be unsettled and entangled. But if thou hast recourse to the everlasting and subsisting truth, thou shalt not be grieved when a friend departs or dies.

In Me the love of thy friend must stand; and for Me he is to be loved, whoever he be that appears to thee good, and is very dear to thee in this life. Without Me no friendship is of any strength, nor will it be durable; nor is that love true and pure of which I am not the author.

Bk. III, ch. xlii.

I have had to drink many a bitter chalice on account of my sisters. David spoke truly when he sang: *Behold how good and pleasant it is for brethren to dwell together* (Ps. cxxxii). But this union is consummated only at the price of much suffering. I did not enter Carmel in order to live with my sisters; on the contrary, I foresaw what a source of suffering they would be if I made up my mind not to give way to nature. Theologians speak of the religious life as a martyrdom. Natural affection is not destroyed; as it becomes purer and more supernatural, it grows stronger, and it is with this affection that I love you, dear Mother, and my sisters. I am very happy to be allowed to fight for the King of kings with my family, but I should be quite content to be transferred by Him to some other field of action. A command would not be necessary; a hint, a mere look would be enough.

As I realized that separation is a possibility, even at Carmel, I accustomed myself to live in Heaven; I accepted the prospect of exile among a strange people not only for myself, but for my beloved sisters. When our foundation, the Carmel of Saïgon, asked for two of them, the question of sending them out was seriously entertained. The thought of the difficulties they would have to face, broke my heart, but I would not have said one word to keep them back.

H.

FEBRUARY 16

Ah! how little is their love of God, how weak is their devotion, who so easily put off the sacred communion! How happy is he, and acceptable to God, who so liveth and keepeth his conscience in such purity, as to be ready and well-disposed to communicate every day, if it were permitted, and he might do it without being noticed.

Bk. IV, ch. x.

During those long and trying weeks I had the unspeakable happiness of receiving Holy Communion every day. Even after the epidemic of influenza had ceased, I was still allowed to continue doing so for several months, although I had not asked for a privilege which was not granted to the rest of the Community.

H.

FEBRUARY 17

My God and my All! Enough is said to him that understands; and it is delightful to him that loves to repeat it often.

Oh! when will this blessed and desirable hour come, when Thou shalt fill me with Thy presence, and become to me *All in All?*

Bk. III, ch. xxxiv.

My soul is filled with the Will of God, so that nothing can penetrate it, but remains on the surface as oil floats on water. If my soul were not already filled, it would be at the mercy of passing joys and sorrows, which succeed each other so swiftly. But these emotions scarcely touch me, and I always enjoy deep peace.

H.

FEBRUARY 18

Dost thou think to have always spiritual consolations when thou pleasest? My saints had not so; but met with many troubles, and various temptations, and great desolations. But they bore all with patience, and confided more in God than in themselves; knowing that the sufferings of this life bear no proportion to the greatness of the glory to come.

Bk. III, ch. xxxv.

Let us work together for the salvation of souls, for we have but the single day of this life in which to give Our

Lord this proof of our love. The morrow will be
eternity, when you will receive a hundredfold in return
for the happiness which you have sacrificed. He knows
the extent of your sacrifice, and that the sufferings of
those dear to you add fuel to your own, for He Himself
underwent this martyrdom for the salvation of our
souls. He saw His immaculate Mother standing at the
foot of the Cross, her soul pierced by the sword of
suffering, and I beg of Him to take pity on your Mother
and comfort her. If those whom you are about to leave
for His sake were to be granted a glimpse of the glory
in store for you, of the many souls who will enter
Heaven owing to your apostolate, they would already
have received the reward of their unselfishness in part-
ing with you.

L.

FEBRUARY 19

Son, always commit thy cause to Me; I will dispose
well of it in due season. Wait for My disposal, and
thou shalt find it will be for thy advantage.

Lord, I willingly commit all things to Thee, for my
care can profit little.

Bk. III, ch. xxxix.

> There is a tree whose roots are fast
>   In Heaven's soil; but see,
> Its leafy canopy is spread
>   On earth! Love is the tree,
> And self-surrender is its fruit.
>   O loving soul, draw near!
> Beneath its shade true peace is found,
>   When love has cast out fear.

P.

FEBRUARY 20

O infinite love, singularly bestowed on man! But

what return shall I make to the Lord for this grace, and for so extraordinary a charity?

There is nothing that I can give Him that will please Him better, than if I give up my heart entirely to God, and unite it closely to Him. Then all that is within me shall rejoice exceedingly, when my soul shall be perfectly united to my God: then will He say to me: If thou wilt be with Me, I will be with thee. And I will answer Him: Vouchsafe, O Lord, to remain with me, and I will willingly be with Thee. This is my whole desire, that my heart may be united to Thee.

Bk. IV, ch. xiii.

If I should be hungry, I would not tell thee: for the world is mine, and the fulness thereof. Shall I eat the flesh of bullocks? Or shall 1 drink the blood of goats?

Offer to God the sacrifice of praise: and pay thy vows to the most High (Ps. xlix).

That is all Our Lord asks of us. He has no need of our works, but only of our love. The same God who declares that He has no need to tell us if He is hungry, deigned to beg a little water from the Samaritan woman. . . . He was thirsty! But when He said: *Give me to drink* (John iv, 7), the Creator of the universe was asking for the love of His poor creature; He thirsted for love.

To this day Our Lord still thirsts. He meets with indifference and ingratitude from His disciples in the world, and even among His chosen disciples He finds very few willing to give themselves up whole-heartedly to the designs of His love.

H.

FEBRUARY 21

Yet this man, thus many ways afflicted, is not without some alloy of comfort for his ease, because he is sensible of the great profit which he reaps by bearing the cross. For whilst he willingly resigns himself to it, all the burden of tribulation is converted into an assured hope of comfort from God.

And the more the flesh is brought down by affliction, the more the spirit is strengthened by inward grace. And sometimes he gains such strength through affection to tribulation and adversity, by reason of loving to be conformable to the Cross of Christ, as not to be willing to be without suffering and affliction; because such a one believes himself by so much the more acceptable to God, as he shall be able to bear more and greater things for Him.

Bk. II, ch. xii.

When I was in the world, I used, on awaking, to think of the happenings, pleasant and unpleasant, that the day held in store. If I foresaw trouble, I began the day with a heavy heart. Now it is quite the contrary; the prospect of difficulties and suffering fills me with courage, and I look forward with joy to the many opportunities I shall have of proving my love for Our Lord and of saving souls, for am I not a mother of souls? So I kiss my crucifix and lay it gently on the pillow whilst I am dressing, saying: My Jesus, You wept and laboured for thirty-three years upon earth. Today You must rest . . . it is my turn to fight and to suffer.

H.

FEBRUARY 22

Oh! how great thanks am I obliged to return to Thee, for having vouchsafed to show me and all the faithful a right and good way to an everlasting kingdom.

Bk. III, ch. xviii.

If you could only realize how tenderly the Sacred Heart of Jesus loves you, and what He expects from you! Your last letter moved me very much, for I saw that your soul and mine are sisters, as you also are being prompted to go to God by means of Love's *lift*, instead of toiling upwards by the rugged path of fear.

I am not surprised that you should find it difficult to live on terms of familiarity with Our Lord: this is not the work of one day. But I feel sure that after my death I shall be better able to help you along this path, and that you will soon exclaim with St Augustine: *My weight is my love: by that am I carried whithersoever I be carried* (*Conf.* xiii, 9).

L.

FEBRUARY 23

But how great each one's virtue is, best appears by occasion of adversity; for occasions do not make a man frail, but show what he is.

Bk. I, ch. xvi.

When we commit a fault, we must never attribute it to a physical cause, such as illness, or the weather. We must acknowledge that it comes from our own imperfection, without becoming discouraged. *Occasions do not make a man frail, but show what he is.*

C.

FEBRUARY 24

When a priest celebrates, he honours God, he rejoices the angels, he edifies the Church, he helps the living, he obtains rest for the dead, and makes himself partaker of all that is good.

Bk. IV, ch. v.

A priestly vocation! O Jesus! how lovingly I would hold Thee in my hands when my voice had brought Thee down from Heaven, with what love I would give Thee to souls! And yet, whilst wishing that I could be a priest, at the same time I envy and admire the humility of St Francis of Assisi, and feel that I have a vocation to imitate him by refusing the sublime dignity of the priesthood. I do not know how to reconcile these conflicting attractions.

H.

FEBRUARY 25

Some there are who keep themselves in peace, and have peace also with others. And there are some that are neither at peace within themselves, nor suffer others to be in peace; they are troublesome to others, but always more troublesome to themselves.

Bk. II, ch. iii.

It is a mistake to want to convince our Sisters that they are in the wrong, even if this is the case, for it is not our duty to correct them. Let us be angels of peace, not Justices of the Peace.

C.

FEBRUARY 26

The whole life of Christ was a cross and a martyrdom: and dost thou seek rest and joy?

Thou errest if thou seekest any other thing than to suffer tribulations: for this whole mortal life is full of miseries and beset on all sides with crosses.

Bk. II, ch. xii.

To live by love is not to rest
  On Thabor's blissful height;
There is another hill I know,
  More precious in my sight:
Love follows the Beloved still
  To Calvary again,
To share with Him the mystery
  Of loneliness and pain.

P.

FEBRUARY 27

I would willingly speak My words to thee, and reveal My secrets to thee, if thou wouldst diligently observe My coming, and open to Me the door of thy heart. Be careful and watch in prayer, and humble thyself in all things.

Bk. III, ch. xxiv.

O Jesus! if I could but make known to all *little souls* Thy unspeakable condescension! I feel that if it were possible to find a soul weaker than mine, Thou wouldst bestow even greater favours on her, provided that she submitted herself with perfect confidence to Thine infinite mercy. My loving Master, why have I this longing to communicate Thy secrets? Thou alone hast taught me; Thou canst do for others what Thou didst for me, and therefore I beseech of Thee to look down in mercy upon a great multitude of little souls. Choose to Thyself a legion of humble victims worthy of Thy love.

H.

FEBRUARY 28

Leave off that excessive desire of knowing; because there is found therein much distraction and deceit. They who are learned are desirous to appear and to be called wise. There are many things, the knowledge of which is of little or no profit to the soul. And he is very unwise who attends to other things than what may serve to his salvation.

Bk. I, ch. ii.

I had always loved what was noble and beautiful, and about this time I felt a great desire for knowledge. What my mistress taught me was not enough, and so I took up various subjects and studied them myself, learning far more in a few months than I had done in several years at school. And yet all this zeal was but *vanity and affliction of spirit* (Eccles. i, 14). For one of my ardent nature, I had reached a dangerous period in my life, but Our Lord did for me as is written in the Prophet Ezechiel: *I passed by thee, and saw thee: and behold thy time was the time of lovers. . . I entered into a covenant with thee, saith the Lord God: and thou becamest mine. . . Thou didst eat fine flour, and honey, and oil, and wast made exceeding beautiful: and wast advanced to be a queen* (Ezech. xvi, 8, 13).

For some time past my spiritual life had been fed on the *fine flour* of the *Imitation*. It was the only book that was any help to me, for I had not as yet discovered the hidden treasures in the Gospel. I was never without my little volume of the *Imitation*, which was a source of much amusement to the family. My aunt would often open it at random and ask me to recite a chapter by heart.

H.

MARCH I

Rest on the Passion of Christ, and willingly dwell in His sacred wounds. For if thou fly devoutly to the wounds and precious stigmas of Jesus, thou shalt feel great comfort in tribulation; neither wilt thou much regard the being despised by men, but wilt easily bear up against detracting tongues.

Suffer with Christ and for Christ, if thou desirest to reign with Christ.

Bk. II, ch. i.

My God, I thank Thee for all the graces Thou hast bestowed on me, and in particular for having made me pass through the crucible of suffering. With what joy I shall see Thee on the last day bearing the Cross as the emblem of royalty. As Thou hast made me a partaker of Thy holy Cross, grant that I may one day be like to Thee, and bear upon my glorified body the imprint of Thy sacred wounds.

H.

March 2

An internal man quickly recollects himself, because he never pours forth his whole self upon outward things. Exterior labour is no prejudice to him, nor any employment which for a time is necessary; but as things fall out, he so accommodates himself to them. As much as a man draws things to himself, so much is he hindered by them.

Bk. II, ch. i.

You become too much absorbed in your work, and worry over it as though you bore the whole responsibility. Do you wonder what is going on at the present moment on other Carmels, and whether the nuns are busy or not? Do their labours prevent you from making your prayer? You must learn to dissociate yourself from your work in the same way, giving the prescribed time to it, but maintaining detachment of heart.

C.

MARCH 3

Thou must not depend too much on this affection, which may be quickly changed into the contrary. When thou hast grace, think with thyself how miserable and poor thou art wont to be when thou art without it.

Nor does the progress of a spiritual life consist so much in having the grace of consolation, as in bearing the want of it with humility, resignation, and patience; so as not to grow remiss in the exercise of prayer at that time, nor to suffer thyself to omit any of thy accustomed good works.

Bk. III, ch. vii.

How sweet and easy it is to serve Our Lord upon earth, and how happy He has made me! He gives me all I want, or rather, He has always made me desire that which He intends to give me. Not long before the beginning of my terrible temptation against faith, I said to myself: I have no great exterior trials, and as for interior ones, Almighty God would have to alter my way of serving Him before that could happen, and I see no likelihood of a change. And yet, I cannot go on living in absolute peace; I wonder what He will do?

The answer was not long in coming, and taught me that our loving Lord is never short of expedients, for without changing the way of my spiritual life, He allows this great trial to temper with gall the sweetness of my consolation.

H.

MARCH 4

Thou, O most sweet Lord, art bountiful to me above all desert, and above all I dare hope or ask for. Blessed be Thou, O my God; for though I am unworthy of all

good, yet Thy generosity and infinite goodness never
cease to do good.

Bk. III, ch. viii.

It is not only trials that Our Lord makes me foresee
and desire. For a long time I had cherished the hope of
having a priest brother, but this seemed an impossibility,
for, having lost my little brothers I could never have this
happiness. And yet, God has even gone beyond my
desire of having a priest brother who would remember
me every day at the altar, for He has united me by
spiritual bonds with two of His apostles.

This is how it came about. My first brother was given
to me as a feast-day present by our Mother, St Teresa,
in 1895. I was very busy in the laundry, for it was
wash-day, when Mère Agnès de Jésus, then Prioress,
took me aside and read me a letter. It was from young
seminarist, who wrote that St Teresa had inspired him
to ask for a sister, who would devote herself to praying
for him and the souls who would be under his care. On
his part he promised to remember the nun chosen every
time he said Mass. I was chosen to be his sister, and the
joy that filled my heart at thus seeing my hopes realized
was unlike anything I had felt since my childhood, when
joy could be too overwhelming for a little heart to
contain. I had never known such happiness for years;
it was as though a stringed instrument long forgotten
once more vibrated to the touch.

H.

March 5

Nature is covetous, and is more willing to take than to
give, and loves to have things to herself. But grace is
bountiful and open-hearted, avoids selfishness, is con-

tented with little, and judges it more happy to give than to receive.

Bk. III, ch. liv.

Our Lord teaches us to: *Give to every one that asketh thee, and of him that taketh away thy goods, ask them not again* (Luke vi, 30). It is more pleasant to give of one's own free will than to be asked, although this is not very hard if the request is politely made. If, however, it is made in a tactless way, a soul that is not firmly established in charity will find a hundred and one pretexts for refusing. If she does finally comply, it is only after having impressed upon the petitioner how inconsiderate she has been, and what a great favour she is doing her. In short, she spends more time in stating her case than she would in performing the trifling service asked of her.

H.

MARCH 6

In some cases thou must use violence, and manfully resist the sensual appetite, and not regard what the flesh has a mind for, or what it would fly from; but rather labour that whether it will or not, it may become subject to the spirit.

And so long must it be chastised and kept under servitude, until it readily obey in all things and learn to be content with a little, and to be pleased with what is plain and ordinary, and not to murmur at any inconvenience.

Bk. III, ch. xi.

I began to feel a real affection for ugly, inconvenient things; for instance, I was delighted when they took away the pretty little water jug from our cell, and gave me an old one, all chipped. I also tried never to justify myself, but this I found difficult, as I wanted to hide nothing from my novice mistress.

H.

MARCH 7

Happy is he whom truth teaches by itself, not by figures and words that pass, but as it is in itself. Our opinion and our sense often deceive us, and discover but little.

Bk. I, ch. iii.

I have never acted like Pilate, who refused to hear the truth. I have always said to my Heavenly Father: I would willingly hear Thee, and so I beseech of Thee to answer me when I humbly ask: what is truth? Grant that I may see things as they truly are, and never be dazzled by them.

N.V.

MARCH 8

This is not the work of man, but the grace of Christ, which can and does effect such great things in frail flesh, and what is naturally abhors and flies, even this, through fervour of spirit, it now embraces and loves.

Bk. II, ch. xii.

Ever since I entered Carmel, suffering has awaited me at every turn, but I have always embraced it lovingly. At the canonical examination before my Profession I said that I had come to Carmel in order to save souls, and above all to pray for priests.

To attain an end, one must make use of the means, and Our Lord having made me understand that it was by the cross that I would win souls, the more crosses I

met with, the more did my desire of suffering increase.
I trod this path for five years, though no one suspected
it. Jesus alone was to be given this flower, whose
fragrance is all kept for Heaven, and so remains unnoticed upon earth.

H.

MARCH 9

Seek true peace, not upon earth, but in heaven; not
in men, nor in other things created, but in God alone.

Bk. III. ch. xxxv.

This is the principal comfort of a faithful soul, so long
as she sojourns afar from Thee in this mortal body,
being mindful often of her God, to receive her Beloved
with a devout mind.

Bk. IV, ch. iii.

> Above the curtain of the clouds
>   Are skies serenely blue,
> And thither, like the lark, I rise
>   Where no care can pursue,
> So near, so near to Heaven's gate!
>   Then to the earth return,
> Where to the hidden Fruit of Love
>   With longing eyes I turn.

P.

MARCH 10

Oh! the lukewarmness and negligence of our state;
that we so quickly fall away from our former fervour;
and are now even weary of living, through sloth and
tepidity.

Bk. I, ch. xviii.

Oh! how little God is loved on earth, even by those
consecrated to Him! No, God is not much loved.

N.V.

MARCH 11

Lord, if Thou seest that this is expedient, and approvest of it as profitable to me, then grant that I may use it to Thy honour. But if Thou knowest that it will be hurtful to me, and not expedient for the salvation of my soul, take away from me such a desire.

Bk. III, ch. xv.

O my Jesus! I love Thee, I love my Mother the Church, and bear in mind that the least act of pure love is more profitable to her than all other works put together. But am I sure that I have pure love in my heart? Are my boundless desires mere daydreams and folly? If this be so, then enlighten my mind, for I only seek the truth. If my hopes are rash, then take them from me, for they are a veritable martyrdom. Nevertheless, should my soul never attain to the sublime heights for which it yearns, this martyrdom, this folly, will have been even sweeter than the bliss of Heaven, unless, by a miracle, Thou didst take away the memory of my earthly hopes.

Jesus! Jesus! if the desire of love be so unutterably sweet, what must it be to possess and enjoy it for all eternity?

H.

MARCH 12

They laboured all the day, and in the night they gave themselves to long prayers; though even whilst they were at work, they ceased not from mental prayer.

Bk. I, ch. xviii.

The Saint always endeavoured to lead her religious life with the perfection that St Teresa expected from her Carmelites. If the work upon which she was engaged was not too absorbing, her thoughts would turn naturally to God. One day a novice entered her cell and was struck by the heavenly expression on her face. She was busily sewing, and yet was apparently lost in contemplation. The novice asked what she was thinking about, and the Saint replied: "I was meditating on the Our Father. How sweet it is to call God our Father!" And her eyes filled with tears.

H.

MARCH 13

Esteem not thyself better than others, lest perhaps thou be accounted worse in the sight of God, who knows what is in man. Be not proud of thy own works, for the judgements of God are different from the judgements of men; and oftentimes that displeaseth Him, which pleaseth men.

If thou hast anything of good, believe better things of others that thou mayest preserve humility. It will do thee no harm to esteem thyself the worst of all; but it will hurt thee very much to prefer thyself before anyone. Continual peace is with the humble; but in the heart of the proud is frequent envy and indignation.

Bk. I, ch. vii.

When I am charitable, I feel that it is Our Lord acting in me; the more closely I am united to Him, the more I love all my Sisters. If I want my love to grow, and the devil brings before my eyes the defects of any particular Sister, I hasten to seek out her virtues and good intentions. If I see her fall into any fault, I say to myself that she may have won many victories which she hides out of humility, and that what seems to me a fault may even be an act of virtue, because of her intention. Having learnt that by experience myself, I do not find it difficult to be persuaded.

H.

MARCH 14

Consider the Carthusians, the Cistercians, and the monks and nuns of divers Orders; how every night they rise to sing psalms to the Lord. It would therefore be a shame for thee to be sluggish at so holy a time, when such multitudes of religious begin with joy to give praises to God.

Oh! that we had nothing else to do but to praise the Lord our God with our whole heart and mouth!

Bk. I, ch. xxv.

How proud I felt when as hebdomadarian I recited the collects in choir! I shared the priest's privilege in saying the same prayers aloud in the presence of the Blessed Sacrament, in pronouncing blessings and absolutions, and, as first chantress, singing the Gospel. The Divine Office was at my joy and my despair, for I longed to recite it perfectly. I am so sorry for the Sisters who forget to give out a versicle or who make mistakes. Sometimes, after having carefully prepared and marked my places, I have had a distraction and forgotten to open my lips at the right moment. Nevertheless, I do not think that anyone could have a greater desire than I have to recite the Divine Office perfectly and assist at it in choir.

N.V.

MARCH 15

If thou wouldst know and learn anything to the purpose, love to be unknown, and esteemed as nothing.

Bk. I, ch. ii.

My little Mother taught me what unsuspected
treasures lie hidden in the Holy Face. Just as she had
entered Carmel before her three sisters, so was she the
first to discover the mystery of love hidden in the sacred
Face of the Bridegroom. When she had revealed it to
me, I understood where true glory is to be found. He
whose Kingdom is not of this world taught me that the
only royal dignity worthy of our ambition is to *love to be
unknown and esteemed as nothing*, and that we should
gladly despise ourselves. I wished that like His, my face
might be *as it were hidden and despised, whereupon we
esteemed him not* (Is. liii). I longed to suffer and be forgotten.

H.

MARCH 16

When the grace of God comes to a man, then he is
strong and powerful for all things; and when it departs,
then he is poor and weak, left, as it were, only to stripes.

In these he must not be dejected nor despair, but stand
with an even mind, resigned to the will of God, and bear
for the glory of Christ whatever shall befall him:
because after winter comes summer; after the night
the day returns; after a storm there follows a great
calm.

Bk. II. ch. viii.

I can now look back upon the past; my soul has been
plunged into the crucible of suffering, and has been
matured by many trials, both interior and exterior.
Just as a flower lifts its head when the storm is over, so
I can look up and realize that the words of the Psalmist
have been fulfilled in me: *The Lord ruleth me and I shall
want nothing. He hath set me in a place of pasture. He*

hath brought me up on the water of refreshment: he hath converted my soul. . . . Though I should walk in the midst of the shadow of death, I will fear no evils, for thou art with me (Ps. xxii).

Yes, the Lord has ever been *compassionate and merciful, long-suffering and plenteous in mercy* (Ps. cii) towards me. I rejoice in this opportunity of singing the praises of His unspeakable goodness, and I am going to write, for your eyes alone, the life-story of the little flower that Jesus has plucked.

H.

MARCH 17

He does much who loves much.

Bk. I, ch. xv.

How can we fear Him who says: *Thou hast wounded my heart, my sister, my spouse . . . with one hair of thy neck* (Cant. iv, 9)? When He speaks of a single hair having such power, He means that the least action done out of love wins His heart. How unhappy would be our lot if great deeds were expected of us, but how fortunate we are to be able to win Jesus by means of such trifles.

L.

MARCH 18

What I have given I can justly take away, and restore it again when I please. When I give it, it is still Mine; when I take it away again, I take not anything that is thine; for *every best gift and every perfect gift is from above* (James i, 17).

If I send thee afflictions, or any adversity, repine not, neither let thy heart be cast down. I can quickly raise thee up again, and turn all thy burden into joy.

Bk. III, ch. xxx.

O tender Mother! thy pure heart,
When Christ thy Son was slain,
Knew the dark night of anguish, the
Extremity of pain.
God asks our all, and we must give
What He did first bestow;
To love and suffer is our joy,
As thine was, here below.

P.

MARCH 19

Protect and defend the soul of Thy poor servant amidst so many dangers of this corruptible life, and direct him in the company of Thy grace, through the way of peace to the country of everlasting light. Amen.

Bk. III, ch. lix.

I had never come into contact with evil, but dreaded the thought of doing so, and I realized that I would come across many disturbing things on my journey. I had not yet learned that *all things are clean to the clean* (Tit. i, 15), that evil is not in material things but in unclean minds. From my childhood my devotion to Our Lady and St Joseph had been one thing, and every day I said the prayer: *St Joseph, father and protector of virgins*. I therefore placed myself under his protection and felt safe from all danger.

H.

MARCH 20

Jesus Christ alone is singularly to be loved. For Him and in Him let both friends and enemies be dear to thee; and for all these must thou pray to Him, that all may know and love Him.

Bk. II, ch. viii.

All that I desire is contained in the following little prayer, which I beg of you to say every day for me: *Most merciful Father, I beseech Thee in the name of Thy beloved Son, of the Virgin Mary and all the Saints, to enkindle my sister's heart with Thy Holy Spirit of Love, that she may by Thy grace draw many souls to love Thee.*

If God should soon take me to Himself, please continue to say this prayer, for in Heaven I shall have the same desire that I have upon earth: to love Jesus and to make Him loved.

L.

MARCH 21

If thou canst but hold thy peace and suffer, thou shalt see without doubt that the Lord will help thee. He knows the time and manner of delivering thee, and therefore thou must resign thyself to Him.

Bk. II, ch. ii.

What is the good of defending ourselves and explaining when we are misunderstood or misjudged? Let the matter drop, and say nothing. If we would only allow others to judge us as they please, how happy we should be! O blessed silence, what peace you bring to the soul!

C.

MARCH 22

Our Lord Jesus Christ Himself was not one hour of His life without suffering: *Thus it behoved*, saith He, *Christ to suffer, and to rise again from the dead the third day* (Luke xxiv, 46).

Drink of the chalice of thy Lord lovingly, if thou desirest to be His friend, and to have part with Him.

Bk. II, ch. xii.

In the Sunday Gospel were these consoling words: *Fear not, little flock, for it hath pleased your Father to give you a kingdom* (Luke xii, 32). My heart was filled with complete confidence, and I felt sure that the kingdom of Carmel would soon be mine. But I forgot those other words of Our Lord: *I dispose to you, as my Father hath disposed to me, a kingdom* (Luke xxii, 29)—that is to say, I have prepared crosses and trials for you, that you may be worthy to possess My kingdom. *Ought not Christ to have suffered these things, and so to enter into his glory* (ibid. xxiv, 26)? If you would sit at His right hand, you must drink of the chalice that He drank.

H.

MARCH 23

Let all teachers hold their peace; let all creatures be silent in Thy sight; speak Thou alone to me.

Bk. I, ch. iii.

The only book that is any help to me now is the Gospel, and in it I find all that I need. I hear Our Lord telling me the one thing I have to do: *Learn of me, because I am meek and humble of heart*, and this brings the peace that He has promised: *and you shall find rest to your souls* (Matt. xi, 29).

N.V.

MARCH 24

If a man give his whole substance, it is yet nothing. And if he have great virtue, and exceeding devotion, there is still much wanting to him; to wit, one thing, which is chiefly necessary to him. And what is that? That, having left all things else, he leave also himself, and retain nothing of self-love.

Bk. II, ch. xi.

The science of love! How sweet those words sound! That is the only science I want to know; having like the Bride of the Canticle given all my substance for love, I *shall despise it as nothing* (Cant. viii, 7). I am so convinced that our love is the one thing that makes us acceptable to God, that it is the only treasure that I seek after.

H.

MARCH 25

O Lord, my God, my Creator and Redeemer, I desire to receive Thee today with such affection, reverence, praise and honour; with such gratitude, worthiness, and love; with such faith, hope, and purity, as Thy most holy Mother, the glorious Virgin Mary, received and desired Thee, when she humbly and devoutly answered the angel, who declared to her the mystery of the Incarnation: *Behold the handmaid of the Lord: be it done to me according to thy word* (Luke i, 38).

Bk. IV, ch. xvii.

> The Lord who made me sheltereth
> Within my mortal frame,
> Just as to Mary, long ago,
> The promised Saviour came.
> O Mary! clothe my poverty,
> And lend me of thy grace,
> That He may find once more in me
> His chosen dwelling-place!

P.

MARCH 26

Deal not roughly with one that is tempted, but comfort him, as thou wouldst wish to be done to thyself.

In temptations and tribulations a man is proved as to

what progress he has made: and in them there is greater merit, and his virtue appears more conspicuous. Nor is it much if a man be devout and fervent when he feels no trouble; but if in the time of adversity he bears up with patience, there will be hope of a great advancement.

Some are preserved from great temptations, and are often overcome in daily little ones; that being humbled, they may never presume of themselves in great things, who are weak in such small occurences.

Bk. I, ch. xiii.

You complain of the very thing in which you ought to rejoice. Where would be your merit if you only made an effort when you felt courageous? It does not matter in the least whether you are feeling brave, as long as you act bravely. If you feel too cowardly to stoop down and pick up a thread, and yet do so for love of Our Lord, your merit is greater than if you had accomplished some great deed in a moment of fervour. Instead of repining, be glad that Our Lord lets you feel your weakness, so that you may profit by it to win souls.

C.

MARCH 27

Thou must be willing, for the love of God, to suffer all things: labours and sorrows, temptations and vexations, anxieties, necessities, sicknesses, injuries, detractions, reprehensions, humiliations, confusions, corrections, and contempt.

These things help to obtain virtue, try a novice of Christ, and procure a heavenly crown. I will give an everlasting reward for this short labour, and glory without end for transitory confusion.

Bk. III, ch. xxxv.

God in His mercy has always preserved me from illusions. I found the religious life just what I expected it to be; no sacrifice took me by surprise, and, as you know, I met with more thorns than roses. My daily bread was spiritual dryness, and, moreover, Our Lord willed that I should be treated with the utmost severity by our Mother, although she did not realize it at the time. Every time I met her I was scolded. I had once overlooked a spider's web in the cloister, and she said in front of the whole Community: *It is easy to see that our cloisters are swept by a child of fifteen! Take away that spider's web, and be more careful in future.*

On the rare occasions when she took me for an hour's spiritual direction, I was scolded nearly all the time. What grieved me most was not knowing how to correct my faults, my slowness, for instance, and lack of zeal in my work.

H.

March 28

O faithful soul, prepare thy heart for this thy Spouse, that He may vouchsafe to come to thee and well in thee. For so He saith: *If any man love me he will keep my word, and we will come to him, and we will make our abode with him* (John xiv, 23).

Make room, then, for Christ within thee, and deny entrance to all others.

Bk. II, ch. i.

> The fox goes somewhere safe to earth,
>   The linnet has her nest,
> The Son of Man can find nowhere
>   To lay His head and rest:
> My heart shall be Thy resting-place,
>   My love shall welcome Thee,
> Thou shalt forget man's cold neglect
>   In me, Thy Bethany.

P.

MARCH 29

If I cannot as yet be all heavenly and all on fire, like the cherubim and seraphim, I will, however, endeavour to apply myself to devotion, and to prepare my heart for the acquiring some small flame of divine love.

Bk. IV, ch. iv.

A few days after I had made my oblation to the All-Merciful Love, I had just begun to make the Stations of the Cross in choir, when I was suddenly pierced by a flaming dart, so fiery that I nearly died. It was as if some unseen force had plunged me into fire. I can find no words to express the intensity of the flame, nor the delight which accompanied it.

H.

MARCH 30

Follow me: *I am the way, and the truth, and the life* (John xiv, 6). Without the Way, there is no going; without the Truth, there is no knowing; without the Life, there is no living.

I am the Way which thou must follow; the Truth which thou must believe; the Life which thou must hope for.

Bk. III, ch. lvi.

In the Gospel of St John Our Lord utters this sublime prayer: *Sanctify them in truth. Thy word is truth* (John xvii, 17). Again, He teaches us that He is *the way, and the truth, and the life* (ibid. xiv, 6). We know well what that *word* is that we must keep; we cannot ask like Pilate: *What is truth* (ibid. xviii, 38)? Jesus dwells in our hearts, and so we possess the Truth.

L.

MARCH 31

What was the reason why some of the saints were so perfect and contemplative? Because they made it their study wholly to mortify in themselves all earthly desires: and thus they were enabled, with the whole interior of their heart, to cleave to God, and freely to attend to themselves.

We are too much taken up with our own passions, and too solicitous about transitory things.

Bk. I, ch. xi.

One Sunday I set out joyfully for the chestnut avenue. It was spring-time and I was going to enjoy the beauties of Nature. Alas, I found that my beloved chestnut trees had been pruned, and the branches, covered with half-opened buds, lay on the ground. It gave me a pang to think that they would take three years to recover from this drastic treatment. Then I thought to myself: If you were in another monastery, you would not in the least mind if they cut down the whole avenue at the Carmel of Lisieux . . . I therefore made up my mind not to worry over passing things, but to walk with my Beloved in the pleasant glades of His love, which no hand can touch.

C.

APRIL 1

I *will confess against myself my injustice* (Ps. xxxi). I will confess to Thee, O Lord, my infirmity.

It is oftentimes a small thing which casts me down and troubles me. I make a resolution to behave myself valiantly; but when a small temptation comes, I am brought into great straits.

Oh! that Thou, the most mighty God of Israel, the

zealous lover of faithful souls, wouldst behold the labour and sorrow of Thy servant, and stand by me in all my undertakings!

Strengthen me with heavenly fortitude lest the old man, the miserable flesh, not fully subject to the spirit, prevail and get the upper hand, against which we must fight as long as we breathe in this most wretched life.

Bk. III, ch. xx.

Dear Lord, Thou knowest my weakness. Each morning I make a resolution to be humble, but by the evening I find that I have frequently given way to pride. If I did not know that it was a form of pride, I should be tempted to discouragement, but I place my whole trust in Thee. Thou canst do all things, give me this virtue which I desire. In order to obtain this grace from Thy mercy, I will frequently repeat: *Jesus, meek and humble of heart, make my heart like unto Thine.*

Pr.

APRIL 2

Love feels no burthen, values no labours, would willingly do more than it can; complains not of impossibility, because it conceives that it may and can do all things. It is able, therefore, to do anything, and it performs and effects many things, where he that loves not, faints and lies down.

Bk. III, ch. v.

Do not grieve at your apparent helplessness. When we begin the day feeling that we have neither the courage nor the strength for the practice of virtue, this is a grace, *for now the axe is laid to the root of the tree* (Matt. iii, 10), because we rely upon Our Lord only. If we fall, we make amends by an act of love, and Jesus smiles once more. He helps us without appearing to do so, and our weak, imperfect love wipes away the tears that wicked men cause Him to shed.

Love can do all things; even impossibilities become easy and pleasant. Our Lord does not consider in the first place whether our actions are great, or difficult to perform; He looks above all at the love with which we perform them. So we need have no fear.

L.

APRIL 3

In peace, in the self-same, that is in Thee, the one sovereign eternal Good, *I will sleep and I will rest.* Amen (Ps. iv).

Bk. III, ch. xv.

During Lent of last year I was feeling stronger than ever, and in spite of the rigorous fast my health kept up to the end, when, in the early hours of Good Friday, Our Lord gave me reason to hope that I would soon go to join Him in Heaven.

I had not been given leave to spend the whole night before the altar of repose, and so I went up to our cell at about midnight on Thursday. No sooner had I laid my head on the pillow than I felt a warm flood rise suddenly to my lips. I felt as though I were dying, and rejoiced at the thought. As I had put out our little lamp, I mortified my curiosity and fell asleep peacefully. When I was called at five o'clock, I remembered that there was a pleasant discovery to be made, and on going to the window I found our handkerchief all stained with blood. I was convinced that our loving Lord had given me a first warning on the anniversary of His death, a faint murmur which told me that His joyful coming was not far distant.

H.

APRIL 4

If I am left to myself, behold I am nothing, and all weakness; but if Thou shouldst graciously look upon me, I presently become strong, and am filled with a new joy. It is very wonderful that I am so quickly raised up, and so graciously embraced by Thee; I who by my own weight am always sinking to the bottom.

Bk. III, ch. viii.

If Thou wilt have me to be in darkness, be Thou blessed; and if Thou wilt have me to be in light, be Thou again blessed.

Bk. III, ch. xvii.

Do not be afraid to tell Our Lord that you love Him, even if you do not feel it; this will compel Him to come to your assistance, to carry you as though you were a little child unable to walk. If the little child is afraid of the darkness and troubled because he cannot see the One who is carrying him, let him close his eyes; this is the only sacrifice Jesus asks of him. By remaining thus in peace, the night will no longer frighten him, because he cannot see it. Soon, if not joy, at any rate peace will be restored to his soul.

L.

APRIL 5

I here offer and present to Thee the excessive joys of all devout hearts, their ardent affections, their ecstasies and supernatural illuminations and heavenly visions;

together with all the virtues and praises which are or shall be celebrated by all creatures in heaven and earth; for myself and all such as are recommended to my prayers; that by all Thou mayest be worthily praised and glorified for ever.

Receive my wishes, O Lord, my God, and my desires of giving Thee infinite praise and immense blessings, which, according to the multitude of Thy unspeakable greatness, are most justly due to Thee. These I render, and desire to render Thee every day and every moment; and I invite and entreat all the heavenly spirits and all the faithful, with my prayers and affections, to join with me in giving Thee praises and thanks.

Bk. IV, ch. xvii.

As for my thanksgiving, at no time do I enjoy less consolation. But that is only to be expected as I receive Our Lord to please Him, not for my own satisfaction. I think of my soul as a piece of waste ground, and ask Our Lady to clear away the heaps of rubbish, which are my imperfections. Then I ask her to set up a tent and adorn it with her own hangings, and I invite all the angels and saints to come and sing hymns of praise. Our Lord seems very pleased with His splendid reception, and this makes me happy, although it does not prevent me from falling asleep or being troubled with distractions, so that I frequently make a resolution to continue my thanksgiving throughout the day, as I have made it so badly in church.

H.

APRIL 6

With two wings a man is lifted up above earthly things: that is, with simplicity and purity. Simplicity must be in the intention, purity in the affection. Simplicity aims at God, purity takes hold of Him and tastes Him.

Bk. II, ch. iv.

> Within these walls the child-like soul
>   Will find her heart's desire,
> Simplicity and love will give
>   Her wings that cannot tire.
> The gentle dove need never fear
>   The cruel bird of prey;
> The soul can, like the soaring lark,
>   Rise heavenwards all day.

P.

APRIL 7

They spent all their time profitably: every hour seemed short which they spent with God; and through the great sweetness of divine contemplation they forgot even the necessity of their bodily refreshment.

They were strangers to the world, but near and familiar friends with God. They seemed to themselves as nothing, and were despised by this world; but in the eyes of God they were very valuable and beloved. They stood in true humility, they lived in simple obedience, they walked in charity and patience; and therefore they daily advanced in spirit, and obtained great favour with God.

Bk. I, ch. xviii.

We are neither lazy nor wasteful; Our Lord took up our defence as He sat at table with Lazarus and the disciples, and Martha served. Mary took no food, but thought only of pleasing her divine Master. Taking an alabaster box of precious ointment, breaking it she poured it out upon His head, so that *the house was filled with the odour of the ointment* (John xii, 3). The Apostles murmured against her, and the same happens to us. Even fervent Catholics consider that we go to exaggerated lengths, and ought to serve with Martha instead of dedicating to God the alabaster vase of our life with all its ointment intact. What does it matter if the vase be broken, so long as Our Lord is consoled, and the world is forced to acknowledge the sweet odour that it contained? It is in sore need of such perfumes to purify the unhealthy atmosphere that it breathes.

L.

APRIL 8

What dost Thou chiefly require of a guilty and wretched sinner, but that he heartily repent, and humble himself for his sins. In true contrition and humility of heart is brought forth hope of forgiveness: a troubled conscience is reconciled; grace that was lost is recovered; a man is secured from the wrath to come, and God meets the penitent soul in the holy kiss of peace.

Humble contrition for sins is an acceptable sacrifice to Thee, O Lord, of far sweeter odour in Thy sight than the burning of frankincense. This is also that pleasing ointment which Thou wouldst have to be poured upon Thy sacred feet, for *a contrite and humbled heart, O God, thou wilt not despise* (Ps. l). Here is a sure place of refuge from the face of the wrath of the enemy. Here whatever has been elsewhere contracted of uncleanness is amended and washed away.

Bk. III, ch. lii.

I had displeased her, and when I went to beg pardon she seemed much moved: "If only," she said, "you knew what I feel! I can understand now with what love Jesus receives us when we ask pardon for a fault.

If I, a poor creature, could feel such tender affection when you came to me, what then must be God's attitude towards the repentant sinner: He will blot out the memory of our sins even more swiftly than I forget the fault you committed, and He will love us more after our fall than before."

C.

APRIL 9

If thou givest thyself to fervour, thou shalt find great peace; and the grace of God and love of virtue will make thee feel less labour. A fervent and diligent man is ready for all things.

Bk. I, ch. xxv.

She was so fervent in her observance that she never forgot the least injunction of the Prioress, or neglected any of the small regulations which make religious life so meritorious. One of the older nuns, who had noticed her remarkable fidelity on this point considered her already a saint.

H.

APRIL 10

If thou wilt be delighted in truth, and receive more abundant consolation from Me, behold, in the contempt of all worldly things and in the renouncing of all those mean pleasures thou shalt be blessed, and an exceeding great comfort be derived to thy soul. And the more thou withdrawest thyself from all comfort in things created, the more sweet and the more powerful consolations thou wilt find in Me.

But thou shalt not at first attain to these without some sorrow and labour in the conflict. The old custom will

stand in thy way, but by a better custom it shall be overcome. The flesh will complain, but by the fervour
of the spirit it shall be kept under.

Bk. III, ch. xii.

I remember that I suffered such violent temptations as
a postulant to indulge myself and enjoy a few drops of
happiness, that I had to hurry past your cell, and to
cling on to the banisters to prevent myself from re-
tracing my steps. There would come into my mind all
sorts of permissions that I could ask, a hundred and one
pretexts for giving way to Nature. Now happy I am now
that in the beginning of my religious life I mortified
myself on that point!

H.

APRIL 11

Well mayest thou be ashamed, if thou hast looked
upon the life of Jesus Christ, that thou hast not yet
studied to conform thyself more to His pattern, although thou hast been long in the way of God.

A religious man who exercises himself seriously and
devoutly in the most holy life and passion of Our Lord,
shall find there abundantly all things profitable and
necessary for him; nor need he seek any better model
than that of Jesus. Oh, if our crucified Jesus did but
come into our heart, how quickly and sufficiently learned should we be!

Bk. I, ch. xxv.

After her haemorrhage from the lungs in the early
hours of Good Friday, she was able to persuade the
Prioress that no harm would come of it, so that the
latter, blind to the gravity of her condition, allowed her

to perform all the penances prescribed by the Rule for that day. In the afternoon, a novice saw her cleaning windows, and noticed that she was deadly pale, and seemed exhausted in spite of her energy. The novice, who loved her, begged with tears to be allowed to ask for some restorative for her. But her young mistress strictly forbade it, saying that she ought to endure a little fatigue on the day on which Jesus had suffered for her.

It was only in May, 1897, that her sisters learned of the accident, and when Sœur Agnès de Jésus reproached her gently for having concealed it from them: "My little Mother," she said, "you can thank God that you never knew! If you had known of my condition, you would have been deeply grieved at seeing that no care was taken of me."

H.

APRIL 12

Know that the old enemy strives by all means to hinder thy desire after good, and to divert thee from every devout exercise; namely, from the veneration of the saints; from the pious meditation of My Passion; from the profitable remembrance of thy sins; from keeping a guard upon thy own heart; and from a firm purpose of advancing in virtue.

He suggests to thee many evil thoughts, that he may weary thee out and frighten thee; that he may withdraw thee from prayer and the reading of devout books. He is displeased with humble confession; and if he could, he would cause thee to let alone communion.

Bk. III, ch. vi.

You grieved Our Lord by not going to Holy Communion, and you distressed me. How astute the devil

must be to deceive a soul in this way! He has achieved
the very thing at which he was aiming. He knows that
a soul that seeks God whole-heartedly cannot be drawn
into sin, so he tries to make her believe that she has
sinned. But even this does not satisfy him, he has
something else in view . . . he wants to deprive Jesus
of another tabernacle. As he himself cannot force an
entrance into it, then he is determined that it shall
remain empty. Oh! to what a sorry plight that soul is
reduced! The devil has won by withdrawing a soul
from Holy Communion, and Jesus weeps!

L.

April 13

Lord, because Thou wast patient in Thy lifetime, in
this chiefly fulfilling the commandment of Thy Father,
it is fitting that I, a wretched sinner, should, according
to Thy will, take all with patience; and as long as
Thou pleasest support the burden of this corruptible
life, in order to my salvation. For though this present
life be burthensome, yet it is now become, through Thy
grace, very meritorious; and by the help of Thy example and the footsteps of Thy saints, more supportable
to the weak, and more lightsome.

Bk. III, ch. xviii.

I was once working in the laundry opposite a Sister
who was washing handkerchiefs, and who continually
splashed me with dirty water. My first impulse was to
step back and wipe my face, so that she might take the
hint and be more careful; but I immediately realized
how foolish it would be to throw away the treasures I
was being offered, and so I concealed my annoyance.
Instead of stepping aside, I made up my mind to welcome all the dirty water that came my way, so that by

the end of half an hour I felt quite a taste for this novel
shower-bath, and was determined to come back again to
this corner where so many riches were freely given
away. So you see, Mother, I am a very little soul who
can only offer very little things to God, and even so,
I often neglect to make the little sacrifices that bring
such peace to the soul. However, I do not lose heart,
but cheerfully endure a little less peace of mind, determined to be more watchful another time.

H.

APRIL 14

Son, now thou knowest these things, and hast read
them all, happy shalt thou be if thou fulfil them. *He
that hath my commandments and keepeth them, he it is that
loveth me, and I will love him, and I will manifest myself
unto him* (John xiv, 21).

Lord Jesus, as Thou hast said and hast promised, so
may it be indeed; and may it be my lot to merit it.

Bk. III, ch. lvi.

*If anyone love me, he will keep my word, and my Father
will love him, and we will come to him, and will make our
abode with him* (John xiv, 23).

> I live by love and ever keep
>   Thy Word within my heart,
> And thus I draw the Father down,
>   Whom none from Thee can part.
> The Holy Ghost, the bond of love,
>   One God in Persons three:
> Till captive in my heart I hold
>   The Blessed Trinity.

P.

APRIL 15

They became needy, and were left in a wretched
condition, who had built themselves a nest in heaven;

to the end that being thus humbled and impoverished, they might learn not to trust to their own wings, but to hide themselves under Mine.

Bk. III, ch. vii.

One day when walking in the garden leaning on the arm of one of her sisters, she stopped to look at a hen who was sheltering her chickens under her wings. After a few moments she said: "Let us go in; I cannot remain out any longer".

When she reached her cell she wept for some time, and was unable to speak. At length she said to her sister: "I was thinking of the figure chosen by Our Lord to express His infinite tenderness. All my life He has done that for me: *He has covered me with his wings!* I cannot tell you what I felt just now. God does well to veil Himself from my sight, to show me only rarely, and as it were *through the lattices* the effects of His mercy, for I think it would be more than I could bear."

H.

APRIL 16

Son, trust not to thy present affection; it will quickly be changed into another. As long as thou livest thou art subject to change, even against thy will; so as to be sometimes joyful, at other times sad; now easy, then troubled; at one time devout, at another time dry; sometimes fervent, at other times sluggish; one day heavy, another lighter.

But he that is wise and well instructed in spirit, stands above all these changes; not minding what he feels in himself, nor on what side the wind of mutability blows; but that the whole bent of his soul may advance towards its due and wished-for end. For so he may continue one and the self-same, without being shaken, by directing without ceasing, through all this variety of events, the single eye of his intention towards Me.

Bk. III, ch. xxxiii.

If my soul were not filled with submission to the Will of God, it would sink beneath the flood of changing impressions, now joyful, now sad, that pour in upon one in this life. They are a great trial, it is true, but they only touch the surface of my soul.

N.V.

APRIL 17

Happy are they who penetrate into internal things, and endeavour to prepare themselves more and more, by daily exercises, for the attaining to heavenly secrets.

Mind these things, O my soul, and shut the doors of thy senses, that thou mayest hear what the Lord thy God speaks within thee.

Bk. III, ch. i.

A child of light am I, who oft
  Neglect to trade aright,
And let my shining talent lie
  Forgotten, out of sight.
The Gospel is a mine of gold
  Love only can explore:
Teach me to find its hidden wealth,
  The secrets of its lore!

P.

APRIL 18

O my God, who art unspeakable sweetness, make me look upon as bitter all carnal comfort which withdraws me from the love of things eternal, and wickedly allures me to itself, by setting before me a certain present delightful good.

Bk. III, ch. xxvi.

A great longing filled my soul: to love God alone, and find all my happiness in Him. I often repeated this passage from the *Imitation* during my thanksgiving: *O my God, who art unspeakable sweetness, make me look upon as bitter all comfort that this world can give!* These words came naturally to my lips, and I said them much as a child repeats, without fully understanding, what someone he loves has taught him. I will tell you later how Our Lord answered my prayer, and how He alone was ever my delight.

H.

When I made this prayer, I did not ask that heavenly consolations might be taken from me, but only illusions and those joys which might draw me away from God.

N.V.

APRIL 19

Dost thou think to escape that which no mortal could ever avoid? What saint was there ever in the world without his cross and affliction? Our Lord Jesus Christ Himself was not one hour of His life without suffering: *Thus it behoved*, saith He, *Christ to suffer and to rise again from the dead the third day* (Luke xxiv, 46).

When thou shalt arrive thus far, that tribulation becomes sweet and savoury to thee for the love of Christ; then think that it is well with thee, for thou hast found a paradise upon earth.

Bk. II, ch. xii.

She had been suffering much pain, and I picked up the book of the Gospels to read her a few verses, and chanced upon the following passage: *He is risen, he is not here, behold the place where they laid him* (Mark xvi, 6).

"That is what has happened to me," she said, "suffering no longer touches me as it did in my childhood; it is as If I had risen and were no longer where I seem to be. Do not grieve on my account, Mother, for now that suffering has become pleasant to me. I no longer feel it."

N.V.

APRIL 20

I became the most humble and most abject of all men, that thou mightest learn to overcome thy pride by My humility. Learn, O dust, to obey; learn to humble thyself, thou that art but dirt and mire, and to cast thyself down under the feet of all men. Learn to break thy own will, and to yield thyself up to all subjection.

Bk. III, ch. xiii.

If today the Saint is able to do untold good upon earth and to bring about a complete transformation in souls, we may believe that she earned this right at the same cost by which Christ redeemed our souls, viz., by suffering and the cross.

The ceaseless war that she waged against her imperious and ardent nature was not the least of her crosses. Even as a child she had formed a habit of never complaining or excusing herself, and at Carmel she wished to be the little handmaid of her Sisters. In her humility she endeavoured to obey them all without distinction.

One evening during her last illness the Community were to sing a hymn at the Sacred Heart hermitage. Although exhausted by fever the Saint went with them, but on reaching the spot was obliged to sit down. A nun made her a sign to stand, which she immediately did, remaining standing to the end in spite of her weak condition.

H.

April 21

Let the Jews seek the glory which one man receives from another; I will seek that which is from God alone. All human glory, all temporal honour, all worldly grandeur, compared to Thy eternal glory is but vanity and foolishness.

O my truth and mercy, my God, O blessed Trinity! to Thee alone be all praise, honour, power and glory, for ever and ever.

Bk. III, ch. xl.

If I humble myself, and acknowledge my own nothingness, and cast away all manner of esteem of myself, and (as I really am) account myself to be mere dust, Thy grace will be favourable to me and Thy light will draw nigh to my heart.

Bk. III, ch. viii.

This is the dream of a grain of sand: Only Jesus . . . and He alone! A grain of sand is so small that there is no room in its heart for anyone else in addition. What happiness it would be to live hidden, unnoticed even by those with whom we live! Oh, my little Mother! I long to be ignored by all creatures. I have never desired human glory, but rather contempt; yet seeing that even this is too great for me, I only wish to be forgotten.

My only ambition is Our Lord's glory; as to mine, I leave it to Him. If He seems to forget me, He is free to do so, as I no longer belong to myself but to Him. He will tire of keeping me waiting before I tire of waiting for Him.

L.

APRIL 22

I am where my thought is; and there often is my thought, where that is which I love. That thing most readily comes to my mind which naturally delights me, or which through custom is pleasing to me. For this reason, Thou who art the truth, hast plainly said: *Where thy treasure is, there also is thy heart* (Matt. vi, 21).

If I love heaven, I willingly think on heavenly things.

Bk. III, ch. xlviii.

Your soul is too noble to become attached to the consolations of this life; you must live in Heaven whilst still on earth, for it is written: *Where thy treasure is, there also is thy heart.* Is not Jesus your only treasure? As He dwells in Heaven, your heart must dwell there also. Our gentle Saviour has long ago forgotten your failings, He sees only your desire of perfection which rejoices His heart. I beg of you not to remain at His feet, but to follow the impulse which draws you into His arms, for that is your rightful place. Your last letter tells me more plainly than ever that you may not reach Heaven by any other way than that followed by your little sister.

L.

APRIL 23

Lift up therefore thy face to Heaven. Behold, I and all My saints with Me, who in this world have had a great conflict, do now rejoice, are comforted now, are now secure, are now at rest, and they shall for all eternity abide with Me in the kingdom of My Father.

Bk. III, ch. xlvii.

O my Jesus! I will fight for the sake of Thy love until the evening of my life. As Thou wouldst take no rest upon earth, I will follow Thy example, so that I may deserve to see Thy promise fulfilled in me: *If any man minister to me, let him follow me; and where I am, there also shall my minister be. If any man minister to me, him will my Father honour* (John xii, 26). To abide with Thee and in Thee, that is my one desire; the assurance Thy words give me enables me to endure this exile, until I see Thee face to face for all eternity.

Pr.

April 24

Although thy opinion be good, yet if for God's sake thou leavest it to follow that of another, it will be more profitable to thee.

Bk. I, ch. ix.

You do wrong in criticising this and that, and in wanting everybody to agree with your views. If we wish to be *little children* we must imitate them, for they do not profess to know what is best, and are pleased with everything. Besides, there is no merit in doing something merely because it is reasonable.

C.

April 25

Nature loves idleness and bodily rest: but grace cannot be idle, and willingly embraces labour.

Bk. III, ch. liv.

One day I was making my way very leisurely towards the laundry to help with the wash, admiring the flowers as I went. The Saint was going in the same direction, but she was walking quickly and, overtaking me, said: "Is this the way to make haste when one has to earn a living and keep a family?"

C.

APRIL 26

Jesus has now many lovers of His heavenly kingdom, but few are willing to bear His cross. He has many that are desirous of comfort, but few of tribulation. He finds many companions of His table, but few of His abstinence. All desire to rejoice with Him: few are willing to suffer with Him. Many follow Jesus to the breaking of bread; but few to the drinking of the chalice of His Passion. Many reverence His miracles: but few follow the ignominy of His cross.

Many love Jesus as long as they meet with no adversity; many praise Him and bless Him as long as they receive consolations from Him. But if Jesus hide Himself, and leave them for a little while, they either fall into complaints or excessive dejection.

Bk. II, ch. xi.

It is not in peaceful repose that Jesus would have us find Him; He hides Himself in darkness . . . And yet this is not how He treated the multitude, for we read in the Gospel that: *All the people were very attentive to hear him* (Luke xix, 28). Jesus attracted weak souls by His divine words, in order to strengthen them against the day of temptation and trial; but how few of His friends remained faithful when He was silent before His judges! The silence of my divine Master is like music to my soul.

A bundle of myrrh is my beloved to me (Cant. i, 12), and we often share the chalice of His suffering, but one day how sweet these words will sound to our ears: *You are they who have continued with me in my temptations: and I dispose to you, as my Father hath disposed to me, a kingdom* (Luke xxii, 28).

L.

APRIL 27

Whilst thou hast time, heap up to thyself riches that will never die, think of nothing but thy salvation; care for nothing but the things of God.

Bk. I, ch. xxiii.

I seem to hear you (her sister Marie) saying: "See what trouble men take to become wealthy; we can amass riches for Heaven much more easily, as though collecting diamonds with a rake! We need only perform all our actions for the love of God."

I would go away feeling so happy, and fired with the ambition to heap up such treasures.

L.

APRIL 28

He is gone before thee carrying His cross; and He died for thee upon the cross, that thou mayest also bear thy cross, and love to die on the cross. Because if thou die with Him, thou shalt also live with Him; and if thou art His companion in suffering, thou shalt also partake in His glory.

Bk. II, ch. xii.

I do not know when my exile will end. I may yet sing the mercies of the Lord for many an evening, but even so, my last evening must come . . . My desire is to die of love, as Jesus died, upon the cross.

E.

April 29

Think not thyself wholly forsaken, although for a time I have sent thee some tribulation, or withdrawn from thee the comfort which thou desirest; for this is the way to the kingdom of heaven. And without doubt it is more expedient for thee and for the rest of My servants, that thou be exercised by adversities, than that thou shouldst have all things according to thy inclination.

Where is thy faith? Stand firmly, and with perseverance. Have patience and be of good courage; comfort will come to thee in its proper season. Wait for Me, wait, I will come and cure thee.

Bk. III, ch. xxx.

We read in the Gospel that the Good Shepherd left the ninety-nine sheep in the desert whilst He sought the one that had strayed. What touching confidence! He can rely on the former, they are held captive by love and would never try to escape. So the divine Shepherd of our souls deprives us of the sense of His presence, that He may bestow consolations on sinners.

L.

April 30

Whosoever finds Jesus finds a good treasure, yea, good above all goods. And he that loseth Jesus loseth exceeding much, and more than if he lost the whole world.

Bk. II, ch. viii.

Lord of the world! in Thee I find
Again those things I left behind:
   The forest and the smiling plain,
   Soft-footed snow and summer rain,
The reeds that whisper in the wind.

P.

MAY 1

No one is indeed richer than such a man, none more powerful, none more free; who knows how to leave himself and all things, and place himself in the very lowest place.

Bk. II, ch. xi.

There is one thing which nobody envies, and that is the last place; therefore, only there can we be free from vanity and affliction of spirit. But as *the way of man is not his* (Jer. x, 23), we sometimes feel a desire to shine. When this happens, we must humbly acknowledge our imperfection, and consider ourselves little souls whom God has to support at every moment. When He sees that we recognize our nothingness and cry: *My foot is moved: thy mercy, O Lord, assisted me* (Ps. xciii), at once He stretches out His hand. But if out of zeal we try to do great things, He leaves us to our own resources.

True holiness consists in humbling ourselves and patiently bearing with our own imperfections.

C.

MAY 2

If anyone, being once or twice admonished, does not comply, contend not with him, but commit all to God, that His will may be done and that He may be honoured in all His servants, who knows how to convert evil into good.

Bk. I, ch. xvi.

Our Lord has given me the grace not to shrink from waging a just war; whatever happens I must do my duty. I take refuge, then, in prayer, and turn to Mary, and Our Lord always triumphs. My strength lies in prayer and sacrifice; they are invincible weapons, and touch hearts more surely than words can do, as I have learnt by experience.

H.

MAY 3

In the cross is infusion of heavenly sweetness: in the cross is strength of mind: in the cross is joy of spirit.

Bk. II, ch. xii.

One of the Community, who doubted her patience, went to see her one day, and noticing her very sweet expression asked the reason. "It is because I am in great pain," answered the heroic invalid, "I have always tried to welcome suffering lovingly."

Another time she admitted: "When I am in pain, or have to endure unpleasant things, instead of looking sad, I try to smile. In the beginning I was not always successful, but now I am happy to have formed the habit."

H.

MAY 4

Oh! how humbly and lowly ought I to think of myself: how little ought I to esteem whatever good I may seem to have. Oh! how low ought I to cast myself down under the bottomless depths of Thy judgements, O Lord: where I find myself to be nothing else than nothing! Oh! immense weight! Oh! sea that cannot be passed over, where I find nothing of myself but altogether nothing!

Where, then, can there be any reason for glorying in myself? where any confidence in any conceit of my own virtue? All vainglory is swallowed up in the depth of Thy judgements over me.

Bk. III, ch. xiv.

The warm sunshine does not harm the little flower, but makes her blossom wonderfully. She still holds the precious dewdrops that one fell upon her petals, and which ever remind her that she is little and weak. If everyone were to overwhelm her with praise and admiration, it would not add a single trace of vainglory to the true joy she feels in her heart when she sees that in God's eyes she is but nothingness.

H.

MAY 5

It is a good counsel, that when thou hast conceived the spirit of fervour, thou shouldst meditate how it will be with thee when that light shall leave thee. Which, when it shall happen, remember that the light may return again, which for thy instruction and My glory I have withdrawn from thee for a time.

Such a trial is oftentimes more profitable than if thou wert always to have prosperity according to thy will.

Bk. III, ch. vii.

You may think that I am inclined to exaggerate the night of my soul. If you judge by the poems I have written this year, I may seem to be overflowing with consolations, a soul for whom the veil of faith is almost rent. And yet, it is no longer a veil, but rather a wall, that reaches up and hides the starry sky. When I sing of the bliss of Heaven and the endless possession of God,

I feel no joy; I am merely singing of that which I wish to believe. I admit that occasionally a little ray of light pierces my dark night, and for a moment my trial ceases; but afterwards, the memory of the light makes my darkness more intense.

I realize better than ever before how tender and merciful Our Lord is; He has sent me this cross when I am capable of bearing it, whereas before I should have given way to discouragement. Now, its only result is that all natural satisfaction is taken from my longing for Heaven.

H.

MAY 6

A certain person, by loving Me entirely, learned divine things and spoke wonders.

Bk. III, ch. xliii.

> John the beloved leaned his head
>   Upon Thy sacred breast,
> And learned the secrets of Thy love
>   No tongue had yet expressed.
> I envy not his favoured place,
>   I too have found Thy heart
> And know its secrets, I, Thy bride,
>   Whom none from Thee shall part.

P.

MAY 7

I have often said to thee, and I repeat it again: forsake and resign thyself, and thou shalt enjoy a great inward peace. Give all for all; seek nothing, call for nothing back; stand purely, and with a full confidence in Me, and thou shalt possess Me.

Bk. III, ch. xxxvii.

Jesus has shown me the only way that leads to the fire of divine love: it is that of a little child who, full of trust, falls asleep in its father's arms. The Holy Ghost speaking by the mouth of Solomon says: *Whosoever is a little one, let him come to me* (Prov. ix, 4), and the same Spirit of love affirms that *to him that is little, mercy is granted* (Wisd. vi, 7). The prophet Isaias reveals to us that at the last day the Lord *shall feed his flock like a shepherd: he shall gather together the lambs with his arm, and shall take them up in his bosom* (Is. xl, 11).

As if these assurances were not enough, the same prophet cries out in God's name: *You shall be carried at the breasts, and upon the knees they shall caress you. As one whom the mother caresseth, so will I comfort you* (ibid. lxvi, 12).

After hearing words such as these, one can only remain silent, overwhelmed by love and gratitude. If other souls, as weak and imperfect as I am, could experience what I feel, not one would despair of reaching the summit of the heights of love, as all Our Lord asks for is self-surrender and gratitude.

H.

May 8

Oh! happy mind and blessed soul, which deserves to receive Thee, her Lord God, devoutly! and in receiving Thee to be filled with spiritual joy. Oh! how great a Lord does she entertain! how beloved a guest does she bring into her house! how sweet a companion does she receive! how faithful a friend does she accept of! how beautiful and how noble a spouse does she embrace, who deserves to be loved above all her beloved, and beyond all that she can desire.

Let heaven and earth, with all their attire, be silent in Thy presence, O my dearest Beloved; for whatever

praise or beauty they have, is all the gift of Thy bounty;
nor can they come up to the beauty of Thy name, of
whose wisdom there is no end.

Bk. IV, ch. iii.

Oh! how sweet was Our Lord's first visit to my soul!
It was like a loving kiss; I felt that I was loved, and in
return I said: I love Thee and give myself to Thee for
ever! Jesus asked nothing of me, no sacrifice. Long
ago He and little Teresa had exchanged looks and
understood each other. On this day it was more than
a look, it was a fusion; Teresa disappeared like a drop
in the ocean, and only Jesus remained as King and
Master. Had she not begged Him to take away her
liberty? She feared it; feeling herself so weak and
fragile, she wished to be united to the divine strength.

H.

MAY 9

Unless I put myself in this disposition, to be willing
to be despised and forsaken by all creatures, and to be
esteemed nothing at all, I cannot arrive at inward peace
and strength, nor be spiritually enlightened, nor fully
united to Thee.

Bk. III, ch. xli.

I said to her: If you continue to live for some time,
no one will be able to understand your illness. She
answered gaily: "What will that matter? Everyone is
free to despise me; that is what I have always wanted,
and now at the end of my life I shall see my desire
fulfilled!"

N.V.

MAY 10

They rejoice without end in the presence of God, beholding His glory face to face; and bring transformed from glory into the glory of the incomprehensible Deity, they taste the Word of God made flesh, as He was from the beginning, and as He remaineth for ever.

When I call to mind these wonders, even every spiritual comfort becomes grievously tedious to me; because, as long as I behold not my Lord openly in His glory, I make no account of whatsoever I see and hear in the world. Thou art my witness, O God, that not one thing can comfort me, nor anything created give me rest, but only Thou, my God, whom I desire for ever to contemplate.

Bk. IV, ch. xi.

We had placed a picture of the Holy Face which she much loved beside her bed, for the feast of the Transfiguration.

"How wise Our Lord was to have lowered His eyes when He left us His portrait!" she said to me. "As the eyes are the mirror of the soul, if we had caught a glimpse of His soul we should have died of joy. Oh! how much good the Holy Face has done me during my life! My devotion to the Holy Face, or rather my piety itself, has been inspired by these words of Isaias: *There is no beauty in him, nor comeliness: and we have seen him, and there was no sightliness, that we should be desirous of him: despised and the most abject of men, his look was as it were hidden and despised, whereupon we esteemed him not* (Is. liii, 2, 3).

I also wished to be without beauty or comeliness, and to *tread the winepress alone* (ibid. lxiii, 3), unknown by all.

N.V.

MAY 11

For the profit of one that stands in need, a good work
is sometimes freely to be omitted, or rather to be
changed for a better. For by doing thus, a good work is
not lost, but is changed into a better.

Bk. I, ch. xv.

During the afternoon she received Extreme Unction
and Holy Viaticum. After the ceremony she showed us
her hands with great respect. She had scarcely finished
her thanksgiving when several of the Community came
to see her and speak to her. She said to me afterwards:
"My thanksgiving was often interrupted, but I remembered how, when Our Lord withdrew into the desert
and the people followed Him, He did not send them
away. I tried to imitate Him by receiving my Sisters
graciously."

N.V.

MAY 12

Thou oughtest often to have recourse to the Fountain
of grace and of divine mercy; to the Fountain of all
goodness and purity; that thou mayest be healed of thy
passions and vices, and be made more strong and vigi-
lant against all the temptations and deceits of the devil.
The enemy, knowing the very great advantage and remedy which is in the Holy Communion, strives by all
means and occasions, as much as he is able, to withdraw
and hinder faithful and devout persons from it. For
when some are preparing themselves for the sacred
Communion, they suffer the greatest assaults of Satan.
This wicked spirit, as it is written in Job, cometh a-
mongst the sons of God, to trouble them with his accustomed malice, or to make them over-fearful and per-

plexed, so that he may diminish their devotion, or by
his assaults take away their faith, if, perchance, they may
altogether forbear the Communion, or at least approach
it with tepidity.

But there is no regard to be had to his wiles and
suggestions, be they never so filthy and abominable; but
all his attempts are to be turned back upon his own head.
The wretch is to be condemned and scorned, nor is the
Holy Communion to be omitted for his assaults and
the commotions which he causeth.

Bk. IV, ch. x.

Remember that Our Lord is there in the tabernacle
just for you, for you alone, and that He is consumed with
a great longing to come into your heart. Pay no heed
to the devil, despise him, and go without fear to receive
Jesus, the God of peace and love.

I can hear you saying: "Teresa does not know in what
a miserable state I am, that is why she thinks as she
does" . . . But she does know, she guesses all, and she
repeats that you can go without fear to receive your only
true Friend. She has also passed through the martyrdom
of scruples, but was given the grace to continue going to
Holy Communion even when she thought that she had
sinned grievously. She saw that it was the only way to
drive away the devil; if he sees that he is wasting his
time, he leaves us alone.

If, as you tell me, you can only find rest kneeling
before the tabernacle, you could not possibly offend
Our Lord so grievously as not to be able to receive Him.
It is lack of confidence that wounds the Sacred Heart.
Pray hard that your best years may not be frittered away
in empty fears. We have only the brief moments of
this life in which to work for the glory of God; the
devil is aware of this, and so tries to make us waste them

on useless work. If you want to be cured, the only remedy is frequent, very frequent Communion.

L.

MAY 13

Hence it comes to pass that all things avail thee little, till thou take notice that I am He who delivers those that trust in Me. Nor is there out of Me any powerful help, nor profitable counsel, nor lasting remedy.

But now, having recovered spirits after the storm, grow thou strong again in the light of My tender mercies: for I am at hand to repair all, not only to the full, but even with abundance and above measure.

Bk. III, ch. xxx.

Finding no help upon earth, in my extremity I turned to my Heavenly Mother, beseeching her to have pity on me. Suddenly the statue came to life; Our Lady became so beautiful that no words could describe her unearthly beauty. Her gentle look was full of tender love, but it was her exquisite smile that moved me to the depths of my heart and made all my woes disappear, whilst two big tears rolled down my cheeks. They were tears of joy. "Our Lady came towards me and smiled, I said to myself; but I will tell no one of this, or my joy will disappear." Then my eyes fell upon Marie, whom I recognized. She was evidently deeply moved, and seemed to have guessed the great favour I had been granted. I owed Our Lady's smile to her touching prayer. Seeing my eyes fixed on the statue, she had said to herself: Teresa is cured!

Yes, the little flower was coming back to life, warmed by a ray of her divine Sun, who had delivered her from a cruel enemy. *The winter is now past, the rain is over and gone* (Cant. ii, 11). Our Lady's flower grew so strong and hardy that five years later she was blooming on the fertile heights of Carmel.

H.

MAY 14

Be therefore always prepared, and live in such a manner that death may never find thee unprovided.

Bk. I, ch. xxiii.

If you were told that you were to die immediately, this very instant, would you be afraid?

"Not in the least. I would be overjoyed to leave this world."

N.V.

MAY 15

It is good that we sometimes suffer contradictions, and that men have an evil or imperfect opinion of us, even when we do or intend well. These things are often helps to humility, and defend us from vainglory. For then we better run to God, our inward witness, when outwardly we are despised by men, and little credit is given to us.

Bk. I, ch. xii.

One year the relations of the nuns and the workmen of the monastery had sent flowers for the Prioress' feast. As St Teresa was arranging them, a laysister remarked irritably: "I suppose these large bouquets were given by your family, so those of the poor must be put in the background!"

The holy Carmelite smiled gently, and placed the humble bunches of flowers in the front row, although

the effect was thereby spoilt. The Sister was so edified
by her virtue that she went to the Prioress and accused
herself of the fault, praising the Saint's patience and
humility.

H.

MAY 16

Give me fortitude, that I may stand my ground;
patience that I may endure; and constancy that I may
persevere. Give me, in lieu of all the comforts of this
world, the most delightful unction of Thy Spirit; and
instead of carnal love, infuse into me the love of Thy
name.

Bk. III, ch. xxvi.

Not long after my First Communion I again went into
retreat for the Sacrament of Confirmation. I prepared
with great care for the coming of the Holy Ghost, and
could not understand how anyone could approach this
great Sacrament carelessly. As the ceremony was postponed, I had the happiness of remaining longer in retreat. Like the Apostles, I waited full of joy for the coming of the promised Comforter, for the day when I
should be a perfect Christian, and bear the cross indeli-
bly imprinted on my forehead.

I was not conscious of the mighty wind of Pentecost,
but rather of the *gentle air* that Elias felt on Mount
Horeb. On that day I was given fortitude to endure
suffering, a gift of which I stood in need, for the
martyrdom of my soul was soon to begin.

H.

MAY 17

O Lord, my God, depart not from me! O my God,
have regard to help me; for divers evil thoughts have

risen up against me, and great fears, afflicting my soul. How shall I pass without hurt? How shall I break through them.

Bk. III, ch. xxiii.

When, tired out by the impenetrable darkness which surrounds it, my soul would take some rest in the thought of eternal life, my torment increases. From the darkness I seem to hear mocking voices which say: You dream of light and of a fair country, of possessing for ever the Creator of these marvels, you hope to emerge some day from the dark mist that surrounds you; go forward then to death, which will not bring what you hope for, but a yet darker night, that of absolute nothingness!

May God forgive me! He knows that I strive to do the works of faith, although I do not feel its presence in my soul. I have made more acts of faith in this one year than in the whole of my life.

H.

MAY 18

If thou wert to choose, thou oughtest to wish rather to suffer adversities for Christ, than to be delighted with many comforts: because thou wouldst thus be more like to Christ, and more conformable to all the saints.

Bk. II, ch. xii.

Would you like to know which are my Sundays and feast-days? They are the days on which God sends me the greatest trials.

C.

MAY 19

Thanks be to Thee, that Thou hast not spared me in my sufferings, but hast bruised me with bitter stripes,

inflicting pains, and sending distress, both within and
without.

And of all things under heaven, there is none can
comfort me but Thou, O Lord my God, the heavenly
Physician of souls, who *killeth and maketh alive, bringeth down to hell and bringeth back again* (I Kings ii, 6).
Thy discipline is on me, and Thy rod shall instruct me.

Bk. III, ch. 1.

The Community is under the impression that you
have always spoilt me since I entered Carmel; *man
seeth those things that appear, but the Lord beholdeth the
heart* (I Kings xvi, 7). Dear Mother, I thank you for not
having spared me. Our Lord knew that His little flower
was too weak to take root without the invigorating
waters of humiliation, and this boon I owe to you.

H.

MAY 20

Who will give me, O Lord, to find Thee alone, that
I may open my whole heart to Thee, and enjoy Thee as
my soul desireth; no one beholding me, nor any
creature interesting me, or at all affecting me, but Thou
alone speaking to me, and I to Thee, as the beloved is
wont to speak to his beloved, and a friend to entertain
himself with his friend?

Bk. IV, ch. xiii.

To live by love is to live Thy life,
    O Joy of the blessed, my King!
Who under a little white host dost conceal
    Thy glory the Seraphim sing.
For Thy sake I choose to live hidden, alone,
    —True lovers a solitude seek —
Day and night in Thy presence my vigil I keep,
    Face to face with my Lord I will speak.

P.

MAY 21

Take courage then, and be brave, both in doing and in suffering things repugnant to nature. Thou must put on the new man, and be changed into another man. Thou must oftentimes do that which is against thy inclination, and let alone that which thou art inclined to do.

But consider, son, the fruit of these labours, how quickly they will end, and their exceeding great reward, and thou wilt not be troubled at them, but strongly comforted in thy suffering.

Bk. III, ch. xlix.

If my life were to be prolonged, I would prefer the office of infirmarian to any other. I would not ask for it, but if it were given to me as an obedience, I should consider myself very privileged. I would do my work lovingly, remembering Our Lord's words: *I was sick and ye visited me* (Matt. xxv, 36). The sound of the infirmary bell should be like heavenly music in your ears. You ought to make a point of passing beneath the infirmary windows, so that the sick may be able to call you and ask some service, as though you were a little slave that everyone had the right to command. If you could but see the Angels watching from Heaven our combat on earth, ready to crown us at the end! If we profess to be little martyrs, we must earn our palm. God does not despise these struggles, all the more meritorious for being hidden: *The patient man is better than the valiant: and he that ruleth his spirit than he that taketh cities* (Prov. xvi, 32).

By the little acts of charity we perform in secret, we convert souls in distant lands, we help the missionaries and obtain abundant alms for them, thus building both spiritual and material tabernacles for Our Lord in the Blessed Sacrament.

C.

May 22

It is a great honour, a great glory, to serve Thee and to despise all things for Thee. For they who willingly subject themselves to Thy most holy service shall have a great grace. They shall find the most sweet consolations of the Holy Ghost, who for the love of Thee have cast away all carnal delights.

O service worthy to be embraced and always to be wished for, which leads to the Supreme Good, and procures a joy that will never end!

Bk. III, ch. x.

If in the midst of our earthly combat and suffering the thought that God has called us out of the world gives us such joy, what will it not be in Heaven, where in eternal glory and endless rest, we shall see what an immense grace we received when we were chosen to dwell in God's house, the very gate of Heaven.

H.

May 23

There is then no sanctity, if Thou, O Lord, withdraw Thy hand. No chastity is secure without Thy protection. No guard that we can keep upon ourselves will profit us, if Thy holy providence watch not over us.

Oh! how humbly and lowly ought I to think of myself: how little ought I to esteem whatever good I may seem to have!

Bk. III, ch. xiv.

The lilies of my soul would droop
And fade, if Jesus went;
The Lily of the Valley, He,
Preserves their spotless purity,
The fragrance of their scent.

P.

MAY 24

The humble man God protects and delivers: the humble He loves and comforts: to the humble He inclines Himself: to the humble He gives grace; and after he has been depressed, raises him to glory.

To the humble He reveals His secrets, and sweetly draws and invites him to Himself.

Bk. II, ch. ii.

When, in order to make it bear before the season, a gardener lavishes care on a tree, he does not leave the fruit upon the branches, but sends it to the master's table. It was with this intention that Jesus lavished graces upon His little flower. He wished to manifest His mercy in me; He who cried out, rejoicing, in the days of His mortal life: *I confess to thee, O Father, Lord of heaven and earth, because thou hast hidden these things from the wise and prudent, and hast revealed them to little ones* (Luke x, 21). Because I was little and weak, He stooped down and taught me the secrets of His love.

H.

MAY 25

A good and devout man first disposes his works inwardly, which he is to do outwardly. Neither do they draw him to the desires of an inordinate inclination: but he bends them to the rule of right reason.

Bk. I, ch. iii.

Keep thyself first in peace, and then thou wilt be able to bring others to peace.

Bk. II, ch. iii.

She taught that the best way to avoid giving way to anger, was to aim at "softening one's heart in advance".

E.

MAY 26

If thou wilt withdraw thyself from superfluous talk and idle visits, as also from giving ear to news and reports, thou wilt find time sufficient and proper to employ thyself in good meditations. The greatest saints avoided the company of men as much as they could, and chose to live to God in secret.

Bk. I, ch. xx.

I worked in silence until the sewing lesson was over, and then, as no one paid any attention to me, I went up to the gallery of the chapel until it was time for my father to come and fetch me. This silent visit was my one consolation, for was not Our Lord my only friend? I could talk to Him alone; conversation with others, even on spiritual subjects, wearied me. Being overlooked by others in this way did sometimes hurt me, but I comforted myself by repeating a verse of a poem my father often recited: *This life is but a ship that bears thee on, and not thy dwelling-place.*

H.

MAY 27

I have Thee in the Sacrament truly present, though hidden under another form. For to behold Thee in Thine own divine brightness is what mine eyes would not be able to endure; neither could the whole world subsist in the splendour of the glory of Thy majesty.

In· this, therefore, Thou condescendest to my weakness, that Thou hidest Thyself under the Sacrament. I truly have and adore Him whom the angels adore in heaven, but I, as yet in faith; they, by sight and without a veil.

Bk. IV, ch. xi.

> *I will not leave you orphans*, Christ,
> The very Truth did say;
> Love holds Him captive still on earth,
> He comes to us each day.
> The snow-white host is but a veil
> That hides Him from our sight,
> For mortal eyes could not behold
> The splendour of His light.

P.

MAY 28

Moses always had recourse to the tabernacle, for the deciding of all doubts and questions; and fled to the help of prayer, against the dangers and wickedness of men. So must thou in like manner fly to the closet of thy heart, and there must earnestly implore the divine assistance.

Bk. III, ch. xxxviii.

The novices, finding that she guessed their inmost thoughts, expressed their surprise. "I will tell you my secret," she said, "before correcting you, I always ask Our Lady to inspire me to say what will be most helpful, and I myself am often astonished at what I teach you. I feel quite sure that I am not mistaken in thinking that Our Lord speaks to you by my mouth."

H.

MAY 29

I am He who made all the saints; I gave them grace; I have brought them to glory. I know the merits of each; I prevented them by the blessings of My sweetness, I foreknew My beloved ones before the creation: I chose them out of the world; they were not beforehand with Me to choose Me: I called them by My grace, and drew them by My mercy.

Bk. III, ch. lviii.

It was on the feast of Pentecost that I told my father my great secret. Throughout the day I prayed for the light of the Holy Spirit, begging the Apostles to pray for me and to put the right words into my mouth. They were the very ones to help a timid child, destined by God to become an apostle of the apostles by prayer and sacrifice.

I seized my opportunity after Vespers in the afternoon, as my father was sitting in the garden, looking at the beauties of Nature. The setting sun turned to gold the tree-tops, and the birds were singing their evening prayer. Through my tears I told him of my hopes of soon entering Carmel, and he wept too! He said nothing to dissuade me, but merely pointed out that I was very young to make so grave a decision. I defended my cause so well, that I soon convinced my generous and open-minded father.

We continued our walk for some time, for I was now reassured and my father's tears were dried. He spoke like a saint, and going up to the wall, showed me some little white flowers like miniature lilies. He gave me one, explaining how Our Lord had cherished it, and made it blossom, and kept it safe. The little flower and little Teresa were so alike, that I seemed to be listening to my own story. I took the flower as a memento,

noticing that all its roots were intact, as though it were
destined to live on in some more fertile soil. My father
had done that very thing for me, by allowing me to be
transplanted from the valley of my childhood to the hill
of Carmel.

H.

May 30

Behold, our King marches before us, who will fight
for us. Let us follow Him like men of courage, and not
shrink through fear; let us be ready valiantly to die in
battle, and not suffer our glory to be tarnished by flying
from the standard of the Cross.

Bk. III, ch. lvi.

For Thee I have a longing desire, and therefore must
sigh after Thee, and cry, and pray.

Bk. III, ch. lix.

There is a passage in the Canticle of Canticles [in the
French] where the bride is compared to singing choirs in
an army encamped, which might well be applied to you.
Through suffering your life has become a field of battle;
for it to be also as *singing choirs*, you must be a harp for
Jesus to play on. But there is something lacking in a
concert if no one sings; if Our Lord plays, then Céline
must sing. To a sad melody she will sing songs of exile;
to a joyful one songs of Heaven ... Everything of
this world, its sad and joyful happenings, will be like
distant sounds powerless to make the harp-strings
vibrate. Only the touch of Our Lord's hands can do
that.

L.

MAY 31

When thou art troubled and afflicted, then is the
time to gain merit.

Bk. I, ch. xxii.

Why are you so happy today? ... "Because I had
two little trials this morning which really hurt. Little
crosses are my little joys."

N.V.

JUNE 1

Nothing is sweeter than love; nothing stronger,
nothing higher, nothing more generous, nothing more
pleasant, nothing fuller or better in heaven or earth:
for love proceeds from God, and cannot rest but in
God, above all things created.

Bk. III, ch. v.

When I read St Paul's description of the different
members that make up the mystical body of the Church,
I could not recognize myself as any of them, or rather,
I wished to be all of them. Charity gave me the clue
to my vocation. I realized that if the Church were
complete in all her members, she could not lack the most
necessary and noblest of all the organs—a heart, and
that this heart was on fire with love. Love sets in motion
all the members, and if it were to die, there would be
no apostles to preach the Gospel, and martyrs would
refuse to shed their blood. So that Love includes all
these vocations, it suffices alone, and being eternal fills
all Time and all places.

Carried away by excess of joy, I cried out: O Jesus,
my Beloved! at last I have found my vocation, my
vocation is Love! The place Thou hast prepared for

me is in the heart of my Mother the Church, where I
shall be Love; and so my dream will come true and
I shall become all things!

H.

JUNE 2

We must be open-handed with Our Lord and give
generously, but let us never forget that He is a hidden
treasure, and that few souls know how to find Him. To
find a hidden treasure we too must hide, our life must
be a hidden mystery. The author of the *Imitation* tells
us: "If thou wouldst know and learn anything to the
purpose, love to be unknown, and esteemed as nothing"
(Bk. I, ch. ii) ... "Having left all things else, he must
leave also himself, and wholly go out of himself, and
retain nothing of self-love" (Bk. II, ch. xi) ... "Let
one man seek this, another that; let this man glory in
this thing, another in that, and be praised a thousand,
thousand times; but thou, for thy part, rejoice neither
in this nor in that, but in the contempt of thyself"
(Bk. III, ch. xlix).

L.

JUNE 3

Thou knowest, O Lord, what is best; let this or
that be done, as Thou wilt. Give what Thou wilt, how
much Thou wilt, and at what time Thou wilt.

Bk. III, ch. xv.

I have always been pleased with what God has given
me, even when I thought that what others had seemed
better and finer.

C.

JUNE 4

Son, patience and humility in adversity are more
pleasing to Me than much consolation and devotion in
prosperity. Why art thou disturbed at a little thing said
against thee? If it had been more, thou oughtest not
to have been moved. But now let it pass; it is not the
first nor anything new; nor the last if thou live long.

Thou art valiant enough, so long as no adversity or
opposition comes in thy way. Thou canst also give
good advice, and encourage others with thy words; but
when any unexpected trouble comes to knock at thy
door, then thy counsel and thy courage fail thee.

Consider the great frailty which thou hast often
experienced in small difficulties: yet it is intended for
thy good, as often as these or such-like things befall
thee. Put it from thy heart the best thou canst: if it has
touched thee, let it not cast thee down nor keep thee
long entangled. At least bear it patiently, if thou canst
not receive it with joy.

                                        Bk. III, ch. lvii.

One day when St Teresa had a high temperature, one
of the Community came to ask her help in some artistic
work which was far from easy. For one moment her
expression betrayed the struggle in her soul, and Sœur
Agnès de Jésus being present noticed it. That same
evening St Teresa wrote her the following letter: "My
beloved Mother, your child has just shed tears of repen-
tance, or rather, of love and gratitude. Today I showed
you my virtue, my treasures of patience! I who know
so well how to preach to others! I am glad you have
seen my imperfection. You did not scold me, although
I deserved it; but as a matter of fact your gentleness
had more effect upon me than sharp words would have
had; to me you are the personification of divine Mercy.

Well, my darling Mother, I can tell you that my imperfection gives me more pleasure than if, by the help of grace, I had been a model of patience. It is such a help to find Jesus just as gentle and loving towards me. I feel overwhelmed with loving gratitude."

L.

JUNE 5

Nothing, therefore, ought to give so great joy to him that loves Thee, and knows Thy benefits, as the accomplishment of Thy will in himself, and the pleasure of Thy eternal approbation. With which he ought to be so far contented and comforted, as to be willing to be the least as another would wish to be the greatest; and to enjoy as much peace and content in the lowest place as in the highest; and to be as willing to be despicable and mean, and of no name and repute in the world, as to be preferred in honour, and greater than others.

Bk. III, ch. xxii.

A rose, that in the morning light unfurled
Its glistening petals to a wondering world,
Is fit, my little Lord and God, to grace
Thy feast. But when, full-blown, its lovely face
Is all disfigured and its petals fall,
Despised, 'tis trodden underfoot by all.
It gladly gave its loveliness, and went,
Its little end achieved, its life well spent.
Take Thou my life, my youth, as they unfold
All their bright promise like a tale untold;
Beneath Thy little feet, there let them lie,
Like petals of a rose that soon must die.

P.

JUNE 6

Give me, O Lord, heavenly wisdom, that I may learn above all things to seek Thee, and to find Thee above all things; to relish Thee and to love Thee, and to understand all other things as they are, according to the order of Thy wisdom.

Bk. III, ch. xxvii.

My way is that of love and trust, I cannot understand those souls who fear so loving a Friend. Sometimes, when I have been reading a book on the spiritual life where perfection is shown all hedged round with barriers, my poor little mind is wearied and my heart dried up, so that I close the book and turn to Holy Scripture. There everything is clear and full of light, a single word opens out a wide horizon before me, perfection seems a simple matter. I see that all I have to do is to acknowledge my nothingness and place myself like a child in God's arms.

I leave to great souls and lofty minds the fine books that I cannot even understand, much less put into practice, and rejoice in my littleness, *for the kingdom of heaven is for such* (Matt. xix, 14). What a good thing it is that there are many mansions in the kingdom of Heaven, for otherwise I doubt if I should ever get there, the way to some of them seems so complicated.

L.

JUNE 7

Confide not in thyself, but place thy hope in God. Do what is in thy power, and God will be with thy good will.

Bk. I, ch. vii.

Thou therefore art the fountain of all good, the height of life, and the depth of wisdom; and to trust in Thee above all things is the greatest comfort of Thy servants.

Bk. III, ch. lix.

How pure one must be to appear before the God of all holiness! Yet He is at the same time infinitely just, and His justice, which terrifies so many souls, is the cause of my hope. Justice does not only consist in punishing the guilty, but also in acknowledging good intentions and rewarding virtue. I hope as much in God's justice as in His mercy, for it is because He is just that *the Lord is compassionate and merciful: long-suffering and plenteous in mercy. As a father hath compassion on his children, so hath the Lord compassion on them that fear him: for he knoweth our frame* (Ps. cii, 8, 13, 14).

L.

JUNE 8

Who has a stronger conflict than he who strives to overcome himself?

Bk. I, ch. iii.

Such a one is conqueror of himself and lord of the world, a friend of Christ, and an heir of Heaven.

Bk. II, ch. iii.

There is a striking passage on bodily penance in the Life of Bl. Henry Suso. He had ruined his health by the appalling penances he inflicted on himself, when an angel appeared and bade him cease, saying: "All this time you have fought as a common soldier; you shall now be made a knight," thus teaching the holy man that the spiritual combat was more sublime than bodily mortification.

God has never let me fight as a common soldier; from the very beginning I was made a knight, and set out on a spiritual campaign against myself, by self-denial and little, unknown sacrifices. I have found peace and humility in this hidden struggle where human nature can find no satisfaction.

L.

JUNE 9

With a full resolution, and with thy whole will, offer thyself up to the honour of My name, on the altar of thy heart, as a perpetual holocaust, by committing faithfully to Me both thy soul and body.

Bk. IV, ch. vii.

Blessed is he that offereth himself up as an holocaust to the Lord.

Bk. IV, ch. x.

That my life may become an act of perfect love, I offer myself as a victim of holocaust to Thy merciful love. I beseech Thee to consume me day by day, and let the flood of infinite love pent up within Thee overflow into my soul, that I may become a martyr to Thy love, O my God!

Made ready by this martyrdom to come before Thee, may it at length cause my death and suffer my soul to pass into the eternal embrace of Thy merciful love. I wish to renew this offering, O my Beloved, an infinite number of times at every heartbeat, until the shadows flee away and I may tell Thee of my love face to face for all eternity.

June 9, 1895.

JUNE 10

Therefore thou must not ascribe anything of good to thyself, nor attribute virtue to any man; but give all to God, without whom man is nothing. This is that truth by which all vainglory is put to flight.

Bk. III, ch. ix.

I think that humility is simply the truth. I do not
know if I am humble, but I do know that I see the
truth in all things.

C.

JUNE 11

Grant me Thy grace, most merciful Jesus, that it may
be with me, and continue with me to the end. Grant
me always to will and desire that which is most acceptable to Thee, and which pleaseth Thee best.

Let Thy will be mine, and let my will always follow
Thine, and agree perfectly with it. Let me always will
or not will the same with Thee: and let me not be able to
will or not will otherwise than as Thou willest or willest
not.

Bk. III, ch. xv.

I had been telling her of the strange power exercised
by a mesmerist over persons who surrender their will to
him. She seemed deeply interested, and the next day
said to me: "Our conversation yesterday was an inspiration to me. If only I could be mesmerised by Our
Lord! That was my first thought on waking, and I
lovingly gave up my will into His hands. I want Him
to take possession of my faculties so completely that
my actions may no longer be human and personal, but
a divine work inspired and directed by the Holy Spirit."

C.

JUNE 12

O holy Father, Thou hast so appointed, and such is
Thy will; and that has come to pass which Thou hast
ordained. For this is a favour to Thy friend, that he
should suffer and be afflicted in this world for the love

of Thee, how often soever, and by whomsoever Thou permittest it to fall upon him. Without Thy counsel and providence, and without cause, nothing is done upon earth.

It is good for me, O Lord, that thou hast humbled me, that I may learn thy justifications (Ps. cxviii, 71), and that I may cast away from me all pride of heart and presumption.

Bk. III, ch. l.

Although the trial I am undergoing prevents my taking pleasure in anything, yet I can still say: *Thou hast given me, O Lord, a delight in thy doings!* (Ps. xci, 5). What could be sweeter than to suffer for love of Thee? The greater the suffering and the less others are aware of it, the more is it pleasing to Thee, O my God! Even if it were possible for Thee to be ignorant of it, I should still be glad to suffer, in the hopes that my tears might be the means of preventing, or at least atoning for one single sin against faith.

H.

JUNE 13

Light eternal, exceeding all created lights, dart forth Thy light from above, that it may penetrate the inward parts of my heart. Cleanse, cherish, enlighten, and enliven my spirit with its powers, that it may be absorbed in Thee, with ecstasies of joy.

Bk. III, ch. xxxiv.

Pauline and I went down to the seashore just as the setting sun was making a broad track of golden light across the water. As we sat on a lonely rock, she explained to me that this was a figure of the light of grace shining across the path of life for faithful souls to follow.

I thought of my soul as a little boat with white sails in the middle of the golden path, and I resolved never to withdraw from Our Lord's look, but to sail straight for the shores of eternity.

H.

JUNE 14

If thou couldst but always continue humble and little in thy own eyes.

Bk. III, ch. vii.

Shortly before her death, we told her that we had been discussing at recreation the responsibility that weighs on those who have care of souls. She summoned up sufficient strength to make this beautiful answer:

"*To him that is little, mercy is granted* (Wisd. vi, 7). Even in the most responsible offices it is possible to remain little. Again it is written: *God arose in judgement, to save all the meek of the earth* (Ps. lxxv, 9) to save, not to judge."

H.

JUNE 15

Difference of thoughts and opinions is too frequently the source of dissensions amongst friends and neighbours, amongst religious and devout persons. An old custom is with difficulty relinquished: and no man is led willingly further than he himself sees or likes.

If thou reliest more upon thine own reason or industry than upon the virtue that subjects to Jesus Christ, thou wilt seldom and hardly be an enlightened man: for God will have us perfectly subject to Himself, and to transcend all reason by inflamed love.

Bk. I, ch. xiv.

She would smile when she saw the novices standing up for what they considered their rights. One of them boasted of having had her idea adopted, but the Saint answered:

"I see you are one of those who stand up for themselves; that has never been my way, I prefer to say with Our Lord: *I seek not my own glory: there is one that seeketh and judgeth*" (John viii, 50).

E.

June 16

Open, O Lord, my heart in Thy law, teach me to walk in Thy commandments.

Bk. III, ch. xxii.

Knowing that *charity covereth a multitude of sins* (1 Pet. iv, 8), I explored the rich mine contained in the Gospel. As I tried to sound the depths of its teaching, I cried out with the Psalmist: *I have run the way of thy commandments, when thou didst enlarge my heart* (Ps. cxviii, 32). Only charity can enlarge the heart. Since its flame, O Jesus, consumes my heart, I have run in the way of Thy new commandment, and will so run until the day when I join the choir of virgins, who follow Thee singing the *new song*, which is that of Love!

H.

June 17

There is no living in love without some pain or sorrow. Whosoever is not ready to suffer all things, and to stand resigned to the will of his Beloved, is not worthy to be called a lover.

Bk. III, ch. v.

Do not imagine that love can be found without suffering, for we carry with us our human nature; and yet, what a source of merit it is! It is our bread-winner, and so precious an asset that Our Lord came down on earth in order to possess it.

L.

JUNE 18

If thou wilt be borne withal, bear also with another. See how far thou art yet from true charity and humility, which knows not how to be angry with anyone, or to have indignation about anyone but one's self.

Bk. II, ch. iii.

I did not always find it sweet and easy to practise charity, and I will tell you one of the many struggles I have had on that score. For a long time I had a neighbour during prayer who did nothing but rattle her rosary, or make some other slight noise the whole time. I may have been the only one to notice it, as I have very keen hearing, but I cannot tell you how tiring I found it. I felt tempted to turn my head and look at the culprit, to make her keep still; but I knew in my heart that it would be much better to endure patiently for the love of God, and at the same time avoid hurting another's feelings. Therefore I did not move, although sometimes bathed in perspiration, and unable to make anything but a prayer of endurance. I wanted to suffer peacefully and joyfully, at least in my inmost soul, and so tried to enjoy this tiresome little noise. Instead of ignoring it—which was impossible—I listened attentively, as though it were a beautiful concert, and my prayer, which was far from being the prayer of quiet, consisted in offering this concert to Our Lord.

H.

JUNE 19

Thy saints, O Lord, who now rejoice with Thee in the
kingdom of heaven, whilst they were living, expected in
faith and great patience the coming of Thy glory. What
they believed, I believe; what they hoped for, I hope
for; and whither they are come, I trust that I also,
through Thy grace, shall come. In the meantime, I will
walk in faith, strengthened by the examples of Thy
saints.

Bk. IV, ch. xi.

What will become of me? Shall the sight of my own
helplessness make me die of grief? Oh no! I shall not
even let it trouble me. My abandonment makes me
dare to remain as I am, fixing my eyes on the divine Sun
until the day of my death. Nothing shall alarm me,
neither wind nor rain; if heavy clouds hide the Sun
of love, if it seems to me that nothing exists but the
night of this life, that will be the moment of perfect
joy, the moment to make hope reach out to its furthest
limit, and, without leaving my place, to know that
beyond the gloomy clouds my bright Sun is shining.

H.

JUNE 20

Fly the tumult of men as much as thou canst, for
treating of worldly affairs hinders very much, although
they be discoursed of with a simple intention. For we
are quickly defiled and ensnared with vanity.

But devout conferences concerning spiritual things,
help very much to spiritual progress; especially where
persons of the same mind and spirit are associated together in God.

Bk. I, ch. x.

Instead of separating us, the grille at Carmel united us more closely than ever: our life was made up of the same thoughts and desires, the same love of Jesus and of souls. The things of this world were never the theme of our conversations. At Les Buissonnets we used to gaze far into beyond the stars, but in the parlour it was our hearts that reached out, and we chose contempt and suffering in this world, that we might enjoy eternal happiness in the next.

H.

JUNE 21

They may indeed sound forth words, but they give not the spirit. They speak well; but if Thou be silent, they do not set the heart on fire. They work only outwardly, but Thou instructest and enlightenest the heart.

Bk. III, ch. ii.

You tell me that my letters do you good. I am glad to hear it, but I do not deceive myself. *Unless the Lord build the house, they labour in vain that build it* (Ps. cxxvi). Unless grace touches the heart, the most eloquent discourse cannot draw from a single act of love.

L.

JUNE 22

Thanks be to Thee, O good Jesus, our eternal shepherd; who hast vouchsafed to feed us, poor exiles, with Thy precious Body and Blood, and to invite us to the receiving of these mysteries with the words of Thy own mouth, saying: *Come unto me, all you that labour and are burdened, and I will refresh you* (Matt. xi, 28).

Bk. IV, ch. i.

Out of Me, both little and great, rich and poor, as out of a living fountain, draw living water; and they who freely and willingly serve Me shall receive grace for grace.

Bk. III, ch. ix.

> All ye who bear a burden
> Come unto Me, Who know
> A place of quiet refreshment,
>   Where living waters flow! . . .
> O Heart, the well-spring of all love,
>   Within Thy depths I hide,
> And drink the living waters
>   That flow down from Thy side!

P.

JUNE 23

What have I then to glory in; or why do I desire to be esteemed? Is it not for nothing, and this is most vain? Truly vainglory is an evil plague, a very great vanity; because it draws us away from true glory, and robs us of heavenly grace. For whilst a man takes pleasure in himself, he displeaseth Thee; whilst he seeks the praises of men, he is deprived of true virtues.

Bk. III, ch. xl.

Oh! what poisonous flattery is daily served up to superiors, what deadly incense! A soul would have to be truly detached not to be harmed by it.

C.

JUNE 24

As soon as ever thou hast delivered thyself up to God with thy whole heart, and neither seekest this nor that for thine own pleasure or will, but wholly placest thyself in Him, thou shalt find thyself united to Him, and at

peace; for nothing will relish so well, and please thee
so much, as the good pleasure of the divine will.

Bk. IV, ch. xv.

> Remember, Lord, my resting-place
>   Is in Thy holy Will;
> Within the shelter of Thine arms
>   My soul shall fear no ill.
> If Thou shouldst sleep, and sudden storm
>   Arise, I'll not forsake
> My peaceful haven; O prepare
>   My soul ere Thou awake!

P.

JUNE 25

If heavenly grace and true charity come in, there shall
be no envy or narrowness of heart, nor shall self-love
keep its hold. For divine charity overcomes all, and
dilates all the powers of the soul.

Bk. III, ch. ix.

As the rule of silence and solitude was strictly kept,
she only saw her sisters at recreation. Had she been
less mortified, she might often have sat beside them,
but she made it her practice to talk to those nuns whose
company pleased her least. No one could tell whether
she had any particular affection for her own sisters.

H.

JUNE 26

I am He that in an instant elevates an humble mind
to comprehend more reasons of the eternal truth than
could be acquired by ten years' study in the schools.

Bk. III, ch. xliii.

God has given me the grace to understand the mysterious depths of charity. If I could put into words all I
know, it would sound like a song of Heaven, but, alas,

I can only speak in halting words like a child. Our
Lord's own words confirm what I say, otherwise I
should be tempted to remain silent.

H.

June 27

The saints that are highest in the sight of God are
the least in their own eyes, and the more glorious they
are, the more humble they are in themselves.

Bk. II, ch. x.

When asked what we were to call her when praying to
her after her death, she replied humbly: "Call me
little Teresa.

C.

June 28

Thou thunderest forth over my head Thy judgements,
O Lord, and Thou shakest all my bones with fear and
trembling, and my soul is terrified exceedingly. I stand
astonished, and consider that the heavens are not pure
in Thy sight.

If in the angels Thou hast found sin, and hast not
spared them, what will become of me? Stars have
fallen from heaven, and I that am but dust, how can I
presume?

Bk. III, ch. xiv.

> Our justices, they are as nought
>   Before Thy judgement-throne;
> Where angels failed, I too would fail
>   If I stood there alone.
> O Thou didst thunder on the mount,
>   Yet love bids me draw near,
> Unite my sacrifice to Thine
>   And banish every fear.

P.

JUNE 29

Fight like a good soldier: and if sometimes thou fall through frailty, rise up again, with greater strength than before, confiding in My more abundant grace; but take great care thou yield not to any vain complacency and pride. Through this, many are led into error, and sometimes fall into incurable blindness. Let this fall of the proud, who foolishly rely on their own strength, serve thee for a warning, and keep thee always humble.

Bk. III, ch. vi.

I understand why St Peter fell. He counted too much on the affection he felt for Our Lord, instead of relying on the strength of divine grace. I am quite sure that if he had said to Our Lord: "Master, give me the courage to follow Thee even unto death," he would have obtained the grace.

I wonder why Our Lord, knowing what would happen, did not say to him: "Ask Me for the grace to accomplish what you desire"? I think it was in order to teach us two lessons: firstly, that His visible presence did not teach the Apostles more than we can learn from the inspirations of grace; secondly, that having chosen St Peter to govern the Church, whose members would include so many sinners, He wished him to learn by experience what man is without the help of God. That is why Our Lord said to him before his fall: *Thou being once converted, confirm thy brethren* (Luke xxii, 32), i.e. tell them the story of your fall, and show them by your own experience how necessary it is for salvation to rely solely upon God.

C.

JUNE 30

Son, cast thy heart firmly on the Lord, and fear not the judgement of man, when thy conscience gives testimony of thy piety and innocence. It is good and happy to suffer in this way; nor will this be grievous to an humble heart, nor to him who trusts in God more than in himself. Many say many things, and therefore little credit is to be given to them. Neither is it possible to satisfy all.

Though Paul endeavoured to please all in the Lord, and made himself all unto all; yet he made little account of his being judged by the judgement of men (I Cor. iv, 9). He laboured for the edification and salvation of others as much as he could, and as lay in him; but he could not prevent his being sometimes judged or despised by others. Therefore he committed all to God, who knows all, and defended himself by patience and humility against the tongues of those that spoke evil, or that thought and gave out at pleasure vain and faulty things of him.

Bk. III, ch. xxxvi.

One day at recreation the portress came to ask for a Sister to do some special work. I had a childish longing to do it, and I was the one chosen. I therefore began to fold our work, but without hurrying, which enabled my neighbour to be ready first, for I knew how delighted she would be to take my place. The Sister who had asked for help remarked laughingly: "You were so slow that I guessed you would not add this jewel to your crown!" The Community all thought I was following my natural inclination.

I cannot tell you how much this little incident helped me to become indulgent. It even prevents my feeling proud when I am judged favourably, for I say to myself: If my little acts of virtue seem to be imperfections, it is quite possible for my imperfections to be considered virtues, and so I say with St Paul: *To me it is a very small thing to be judged by you, or by man's day; but neither do I judge my own self. For I am not conscious to myself of anything, yet am I not hereby justified, but he that judgeth me is the Lord* (I Cor. iv, 3, 4).

H.

JULY 1

Wherein then can I hope, or in what must I put my trust, but in God's great mercy alone, and in the hope of heavenly grace?

Bk. II, ch. ix.

In te Domine speravi (In thee, O Lord, have I hoped). How happy I was when it was my turn to recite this verse in choir at the time of our great family trial!

N.V.

JULY 2

If thou set thyself to what thou oughtest; that is, to suffer and die to thyself, it will quickly be better for thee, and thou shalt find peace.

Bk. II, ch. xii.

I had made what I considered an act of heroic virtue, and expected her to congratulate me, but she only said: "What is this little act of virtue compared with what Our Lord has the right to expect from you? You ought rather to feel humbled at missing so many opportunities of proving your love."

I was not best pleased by this remark, and waited to see how the Saint would behave in some trying situation. I soon had an occasion, for Mother Prioress having asked us to do a difficult and exacting piece of work, I deliberately added to the difficulty, without once finding her at fault, but always gracious and cheerful, not sparing herself. If it was a question of helping others and putting herself out, she at once seized the opportunity with alacrity.

At last I could stand it no longer, and putting my arms round her I told her what had been troubling my mind. "How do you manage," I asked her, "always to remain happy, peaceful and even?"

"I was not always like that," she said, "but ever since I gave up all self-seeking, I have led the happiest of lives."

C.

JULY 3

Christ was also in this world despised by men, and in His greatest necessity forsaken by His acquaintance and friends, in the midst of reproaches. Christ would suffer and be despised; and dost thou dare to complain of anyone?

Bk. II, ch. i.

> Thy lot on earth was open scorn,
>   So let it, Lord, be mine.
> To men, the lowest place is shame;
> But since to it Thy meekness came,
>   Thou makest it divine.

P.

JULY 4

The other is that of the divine law, containing holy doctrine, teaching the right faith, and firmly leading even within the veil, where is the Holy of holies. Thanks be to Thee, O Lord Jesus, Light of eternal Light, for the table of holy doctrine which Thou hast afforded us by the ministry of Thy servants, the prophets, and apostles, and other teachers.

Bk. IV, ch. xi.

I feel that I am about to begin my mission to make others love God as I have loved Him, and of teaching souls my little way. If my desire is granted, I shall spend my Heaven until the last day doing good upon earth. This cannot be impossible, for the angels enjoy the beatific vision and yet watch over us. I cannot rest as long as there are souls to save, but at the end of the world when the Angel will proclaim that *Time shall be no longer* (Apoc. x, 6), then I shall rest and be happy, for the number of the elect will be made up, and all will have entered into joy and peace. My soul exults at the thought.   N.V.

JULY 5

What is it thou sayest, my son? Cease to complain, considering My Passion, and the suffering of the saints. Thou hast not yet resisted unto blood. What thou sufferest is but little, in comparison to them who have suffered so much, who have been so strongly tempted, so grievously afflicted, so many ways tried and exercised. Thou must then call to mind the heavy sufferings of others, that thou mayest the easier bear the little things thou sufferest. And if to thee they seem not little, take heed lest this also proceed from thine impatience.

Bk. III, ch. xix.

One day I complained of being more tired than the other Sisters, because in addition to a Community duty I had done some work of which no one knew. The Servant of God replied: "I would like to see you a brave soldier who never speaks of his own troubles, who considers the wounds of his comrades serious, but his own mere scratches. Why are you feeling your fatigue so much? It is because no one knows of it."

C.

JULY 6

Oh, how good a thing and how peaceable it is to be silent of others, nor to believe all that is said, nor easily to report what one has heard!

Bk. III, ch. xlv.

The first infirmarian, a senior nun, had through forgetfulness neglected a duty. As this might have had serious consequences for the patient, the Prioress asked for an explanation: "I was obliged to tell our Mother the whole truth," said the Saint, "but it came into my mind to word the explanation more charitably than I had at first thought of doing. I followed the inspiration, and God rewarded me with deep interior peace."

N.V.

JULY 7

A true lover of Christ and a diligent pursuer of virtue does not hunt after comforts, nor seek such sensible sweetnesses; but is rather willing to bear strong trials and hard labours for Christ. For heavenly comfort is promised to such as have been proved by temptation. *To him that overcometh*, saith Our Lord, *I will give to eat of the tree of life* (Apoc. ii, 7).

Bk. II, ch. ix.

From a pure heart proceeds the fruit of a good life.

Bk. III, ch. xxxi.

Make the sacrifice to God of never gathering fruit; that is to say, of always feeling dislike for suffering and humiliation, of seeing the blossom of your desires and your good will fall to the ground without ever producing fruit during your lifetime. At the moment of your death, in the twinkling of an eye, God will make ripe fruit appear on the tree of your soul.

C.

JULY 8

This is not the work of man, but the grace of Christ, which can and does effect such great things in frail flesh; and what it naturally abhors and flies, even this, through fervour of spirit, it now embraces and loves.

Bk. II, ch. xii.

Her spirit of self-sacrifice had become universal. She hastened to claim as her share anything that was hard or distasteful. Whatever God asked of her, she gave, without a thought of self.

H.

JULY 9

Ah! Lord God, when shall I be wholly united to, and absorbed in Thee, and altogether forgetful of myself? Thou in me, and I in Thee; and so grant us both to continue in one. Verily, Thou art my Beloved, the choicest amongst thousands, in whom my soul is well pleased to dwell all the days of her life. O infinite love, singularly bestowed upon man!

Bk. IV, ch. xiii.

Love attracts love, and mine longs to fill the depths which draw it, but alas, it is like a dew-drop lost in the ocean! To love Thee in return as I ought, I must have recourse to Thine own love, and only then can I rest. O Jesus! surely it is impossible for any soul to be loved more than mine has been! This gives me confidence to ask that Thou mayest love those Thou hast given me,

even as Thou hast loved me. If in Heaven I discover
that Thou hast loved them more, I shall rejoice, for
even on earth I realized that they deserved more. Nevertheless, I cannot now conceive of anything greater than
the boundless love Thou hast poured out upon me,
without my having in any way deserved it.

H.

JULY 10

They indeed advance most of all others in virtue who
strive manfully to overcome those things which they
find more troublesome or contrary to them. For there a
man makes greater progress and merits greater grace,
where he overcomes himself more, and mortifies himself in spirit.

Bk. I, ch. xxv.

How I would have loved the office of infirmarian!
I know it requires great self-denial, but the thought of
Our Lord's words: *I was sick and you visited me* (Matt.
xxv, 36), would have inspired me to do the work with
love.

"Now you have to carry round little cups," she said
to a novice to encourage her, "but soon it will be Our
Lord's turn, for He says that *passing he will minister unto
them*" (Luke xii, 36).

E.

JULY 11

How little soever it be, if a thing be inordinately
loved and regarded, it keeps thee back from the Sovereign Good, and corrupts the soul.

Bk. III, ch. xlii.

I had been asked for a pin to which I was much

attached, as it was so useful. "Oh!" said the Saint to me, "you are too rich to be happy!"

C.

JULY 12

Nature has regard to temporal things, rejoices at earthly gain, is troubled at losses, and is provoked at every slight injurious word: but grace attends to things eternal, and cleaves not to those which pass with time; neither is she disturbed at the loss of things, nor exasperated with hard words, for she places her treasure and her joy in heaven, where nothing is lost.

Bk. III, ch. liv.

Our Lord does not wish me to claim what is mine: I should take this as a matter of course, for nothing really belongs to me, and I ought to be glad to feel poverty because of the solemn vow I have taken. I used to think I was detached from everything, but now that Our Lord's words have been made so clear to me, I see how imperfect I am. If, for instance, I sit down to paint and find the paint-brushes in disorder, or that the ruler or pen-knife have disappeared, I am sorely tempted to give way to impatience, and I have to hold myself back from calling out sharply for the missing articles.

I may certainly ask for what I need; if I do it humbly, I am not disobeying Our Lord. On the contrary, I am acting like a beggar who stretches out his hand and does not take it amiss if he is refused an alms, for he has no rights. Oh! what peace fills the soul that rises above mere natural feelings! There is no joy like that felt by the truly poor in spirit. If in a spirit of detachment she asks for what she needs, and not only meets with a refusal, but must give up what she has, she is only following Our Lord's counsel: *If a man contend with thee in judgement, and take away thy coat, let go thy cloak also unto him* (Matt. v, 40).

H.

JULY 13

If thou hadst a good conscience, thou wouldst not much fear death.

Bk. I, ch. xxiii.

"So death will come to fetch you?" "No, not death, but God Himself. Death is not the horrible spectre we see represented in pictures. The catechism teaches that death is the separation of the soul from the body; that is all. I am not afraid of a separation which will unite me for ever with God."

C.

JULY 14

Thy cell, if thou continue in it, grows sweet; but if thou keep not to it, it becomes tedious and distrasteful. If, in the beginning of thy conversion, thou accustom thyself to remain in thy cell, and keep it well, it will be to thee afterwards a dear friend and a most agreeable delight.

Bk. I, ch. xx.

At the beginning of July her condition became serious, and she was taken down to the infirmary. Looking at her empty cell and knowing that she would never return, Mère Agnès de Jésus said to her: "How painful it will be to see this cell after you have been taken from us!" "My little Mother, you must comfort yourself with the thought of my happiness in Heaven, which in great measure I shall have earned in this little cell. I have suffered so much here, that I would have been glad also to die here."

H.

JULY 15

If thou wilt enter into life, keep the commandments (Matt. xix, 17). If thou wilt know the truth, believe Me: if thou wilt be perfect, sell all: if thou wilt be My disciple, deny thyself: if thou wilt possess a blessed life, despise this present life.

Bk. III, ch. lvi.

> O Poverty! thy faithful hands
>   Have stripped me for the race,
> The snare is broken that did hold
>   Me fast, but for thy grace.
> Let others cling to joys that bring
>   But weariness and pain;
> I run my course, unfettered, free,
>   Eternal joy to gain.

P.

JULY 16

They are all one through the bond of love; they have the same sentiments, the same will, and all mutually love one another. For being elevated above themselves and drawn out of the love of themselves, they are wholly absorbed in the love of Me, in whom also they rest by an eternal enjoyment. Nor is there anything which can divert them from Me, or depress them: for being full of the eternal truth, they burn with the fire of a charity that cannot be extinguished.

In many there is ignorance, especially in such as being but little enlightened seldom know how to love anyone with a perfect spiritual love. They are as yet much inclined to such or such by a natural affection and human friendship. But there is an incomparable distance between what the imperfect imagine, and what enlightened men contemplate by revelation from above.

Bk. III, ch. lviii.

One of the greatest graces I have received this year has been to understand in all its implications the law of charity. I had never fully grasped Our Lord's meaning when He said: *The second is like to this: thou shalt love thy neighbour as thyself* (Matt. xxii, 39). I applied myself chiefly to the love of God, and it was in loving Him that I learned the true meaning of these words: *Not everyone that saith to me, Lord, Lord, shall enter into the kingdom of heaven: but he that doth the will of my Father who is in heaven, he shall enter into the kingdom of heaven* (Matt. vii, 21).

I learned what is the will of God from Our Lord's words at the Last Supper, when in giving them His *new commandment* He bade them love one another as He had loved them (John xii, 34). I began to study in what way He had loved them; evidently not for their natural qualities, for they were ignorant, and did not look at things from a supernatural point of view. Yet Our Lord calls them His friends, His brethren; wishes them to share with Him the kingdom of Heaven. He throws open the way to Heaven by dying for them upon the Cross, saying: *Greater love than this no man hath, that a man lay down his life for his friends* (John xv, 13).

H.

JULY 17

Be never altogether idle; but either reading, or writing, or praying, or meditating, or labouring in something that may be for the common good.

Bk. I, ch. xix.

I told the Saint how it surpised me never to find her idle, although so ill. "I always feel the need," she said, "of having some work in hand. It prevents my thinking about myself and wasting time."

N.V.

JULY 18

The devil never sleeps, neither is the flesh yet dead: therefore thou must not cease to prepare thyself for battle, for on the right hand and on the left are enemies that never rest.

Bk. II, ch. ix.

For several days she had suffered great mental anguish, and often implored us to pray and get prayers said for her: "If one only knew how necessary it is to pray for those in their agony! How much we need that verse of the hymn at Compline: *Procul recedant somnia et noctium phantasmata* (Far off let idle visions fly; no phantom of the night molest)! I think the devil must have obtained permission from Almighty God to tempt me by the extremity of my suffering to fail in patience and faith."

N.V.

JULY 19

Love is swift, sincere, pious, pleasant and delightful; strong, patient, faithful, prudent, long-suffering, courageous, and never seeking itself: for where a man seeks himself, there he falls from love.

Bk. III, ch. v.

I had noticed that Mother Prioress seemed to take special pleasure in talking to one member of the Community, and apparently liked and trusted her more than she did me. I told the Saint how this hurt me, expecting sympathy, but to my astonishment she said: "No doubt you think that you love our Mother very much?" "Of course! Otherwise I should not mind if others were preferred to me." "Very well; I will show you that you are making a mistake; you do not love her but yourself. When we really love someone, we rejoice at their happiness and would make any sacrifice to secure it. If you loved our Mother sincerely and unselfishly for her own sake, you would be glad if she found pleasure even at the expense of your own feelings. Therefore, if you see that she prefers talking to others rather than to you, do not be hurt by this apparent neglect."

C.

JULY 20

Lord, I will suffer willingly for Thee whatsoever Thou art pleased should befall me. I will receive with indifference from Thy hand good and evil, sweet and bitter, joy and sorrow; and will give Thee thanks for all that happens to me.

Bk. III, ch. xvii.

"They say of you that you have never suffered much." With a smile she pointed to a glass containing a draught of a bright red colour: "To look at it," she said, "one would think it a delicious drink, yet it is exceedingly bitter. It is a figure of my life; to others it has seemed bright and happy, as though I drank from the cup of delight, yet all the while it was most bitter. I speak of bitterness, but my life has not been embittered, for I knew how to draw joy and comfort from it all."

H.

JULY 21

Let not therefore thy heart be troubled, and let it not fear. Believe in Me and trust in My mercy.

Bk. III, ch. xxx.

Having received so many graces, I can cry out with the Psalmist: *Give praise to the Lord, for he is good: for his mercy endureth for ever* (Ps. cxvii). I cannot help thinking that if everyone were given such graces, no one would fear God, but all would love Him with a boundless love. No longer out of fear, but out of love no soul would deliberately commit the least fault.

H.

JULY 22

Thou showest me to myself, what I am, what I have been, and what I am come to: for I am nothing, and I knew it not. If I am left to myself, behold I am nothing, and all weakness; but it is very wonderful that I am so quickly raised up, and so graciously embraced by Thee.

It is Thy love that effects this, freely preventing me and assisting me in so many necessities; preserving me also from grievous dangers, and, as I may truly say, delivering me from innumerable evils.

Bk. III, ch. viii.

Our Lord knew that I was too weak to be exposed to temptation; I would have burnt my wings in the flame of this world, so I was not shown its deceptive light. Where strong souls finds happiness, yet deny themselves out of fidelity, I find only suffering. What merit, then, can I claim for not having fallen a victim to such attachments, when it was the mercy of God that prevented me? Without Him I could have fallen as low as

St Mary Magdalen, and His grave words to Simon the Pharisee stir me to the depths of my soul. I know that *to whom less is forgiven, he loveth less* (Luke vii, 47), and yet I have been forgiven more than was St Mary Magdalen.

It is difficult to explain what I mean, but the following example will help: supposing the son of a clever doctor stumbles over a stone on the road and breaks a limb. His father hastens to him, lifts him up lovingly and attends to his injury, making use of his medical skill. When cured, his son will show his gratitude, having every reason to love so kind a father. Here is another example: the father, knowing there is a dangerous obstacle in his son's path, goes on ahead and, unseen by anyone, removes it. The son, not knowing what he owes to his father's foresight, naturally does not express his gratitude, and loves him less than he would if cured of a serious injury. If, however, he comes to hear of it, he will love his father more than before.

I am the privileged child of God's loving Providence, of the Father who sent His Word *not to call the just, but sinners* (Luke v, 32). He expects me to love Him, not because He has forgiven me *much*, but because He has forgiven me *all*. Before receiving any proof of my love such as St Mary Magdalen gave, He let me know how much He had shielded and loved me, that I might love Him with my whole heart in return. I have often heard it said at retreats and at other times that no innocent soul loves more than a repentant one, but I long to prove this untrue.

H.

July 23

When thou thinkest I am far from thee, I am often nearest to thee. When thou judgest that almost all is lost, then oftentimes it is that thou art in the way of the greatest gain of merit. All is not lost when anything falls out otherwise than thou wouldst have it.

Thou must not judge according to thy present feeling; nor give thyself up in such manner to any trouble, from whencesoever it comes; nor take it so, as if all hope were gone of being delivered out of it.

Bk. III, ch. xxx.

"All is not lost, my dear child," the Bishop said to me, "but I am glad that you are going to Rome with your father; the journey will make your vocation all the stronger."

So we had to return to Lisieux without having obtained a favourable answer. My future seemed hopeless; as I advanced towards my goal, the difficulties in the way seemed to increase. In spite of them, my soul was in great peace, for I only sought the Will of God.

H.

JULY 24

Then the flesh that has been mortified shall triumph more than if it had always been pampered in delights. Then shall the mean habit shine, and fine clothing appear contemptible.

Bk. I, ch. xxiv.

Someone had pitied the Carmelites for having to wear thick habits in hot weather: "In Heaven," said the Saint, "God will reward us for having worn thick and heavy habits for love of Him."

N.V.

JULY 25

Thou oughtest indeed to be so far dead to such affections of persons beloved, as to wish, as far as appertains to thee, to be without any company of man.

Learn, for the Creator's sake, to overcome thyself in all things; and then thou shalt be able to attain to the knowledge of God.

Bk. III, ch. xlii.

"Supposing one of us (her three sisters) had been ill in your place, would you have come to the infirmary during recreation?"

"I should have gone straight to recreation without asking how you were, taking good care, however, not to draw attention to my sacrifice. If I had been sent to the infirmary, I should have gone with a pure intention, to give you pleasure and not to please myself. In that way you would have been given graces that would have been withheld if I had been merely selfish, and for my part I would have drawn strength from my self-denial. If, out of human frailty, I sometimes acted otherwise, without feeling discouraged I would try to make up for my failings by greater self-denial unsuspected by others."

N.V.

JULY 26

O my God, my eternal Love, my whole Good, and never-ending Happiness, I desire to reserve nothing to myself, but freely and most willingly to sacrifice myself and all that is mine to Thee. O Lord, my God, my Creator and Redeemer, I also wish to be inflamed with great and holy desires, and to present myself to Thee with my whole heart.

Receive my wishes, O Lord my God, and my desires of giving Thee infinite praise. These I render, and desire to render Thee every day and every moment.

Bk. IV, ch. xvii.

"I think that Love's victims will not be judged, but that God will bestow eternal happiness on them immediately, because of the fire of His love which He sees burning in their hearts."

"To obtain this privilege, do you think it is enough to make the Act of Oblation that you drew up?"

"Oh, no! words are not enough ... To be a victim of love, you must surrender yourself entirely. One is consumed by love only in the measure that one gives oneself up to Love."

C.

JULY 27

If thou thinkest rightly and considerest things in truth, thou oughtest never to be so much dejected and troubled for any adversity: but rather to rejoice and give thanks: yea, to account this as a special subject of joy, that afflicting thee with sorrows, I do not spare thee.

Bk. III, ch. xxx.

Do not think that you will have nothing but happiness when I am in Heaven; that is not what I have had, nor what I have wanted. You may, on the contrary, have great trials, but I will obtain light for you to appreciate and love them. You will be compelled to say as I do: *Thou hast given me, O Lord, a delight in thy doings* (Ps. xci).

N.V.

JULY 28

He does well who regards rather the common good than his own will. That seems often to be charity which is rather natural affection; because our own natural inclination, self-will, hope of retribution, desire of our own interest, will seldom be wanting. He that has true and perfect charity seeks himself in no one thing, but desires only the glory of God in all things.

Bk. I, ch. xv.

"You will find more opportunities of practising virtue at recreation than at any other time. If you want to gain merit, go with the intention of recreating others, not yourself, in a spirit of detachment. If, for instance, you begin to tell your neighbour what seems to you an interesting story, and she interrupts you with a story of her own that does not interest you, listen to her and do not try to bring back the conversation to your original remark. If you do this, you will go away from recreation with deep inward peace and renewed strength for the practice of virtue, because you did not seek your own satisfaction, but tried to give pleasure to others. If you only knew how much you gain by denying yourself on all occasions!"

"You know it well; I think it is what you have always done."

"Yes, I have always tried to forget myself and not to seek my own satisfaction."

C.

JULY 29

They are all one through the bond of love; they have the same sentiments, the same will, and all mutually love one another.

Bk. III, ch. lviii.

Take, O Lord, from our hearts all jealousy, indignation, wrath, and contention, and whatsoever may hurt charity, and lessen brotherly love.

Bk. IV, ch. ix.

She spoke of the Communion of Saints, and explained that what one possessed would be shared by all: "Just as a mother is proud of her children, so we shall be proud of one another without the least trace of jealousy."

N.V.

JULY 30

If thou hadst a right spirit within thee, and wert purified from earthly affections, all things would turn to thy good and to thy profit. For this reason do many things displease thee, and often trouble thee, because thou art not as yet perfectly dead to thyself, nor separated from all earthly things.

Bk. II, ch. i.

It is true that I am not always faithful, but I do not give way to discouragement; I just place myself in Our Lord's arms, and He teaches me to draw profit from both the good and the bad in me. He shows me how to gamble on the bank of love, or rather, He makes all the investments without consulting me. It is not my concern to know how much I am winning; what I have to do is to give myself entirely to Him. After all, I am no prodigal, there is no need for Him to prepare a feast for me, *because I am always with him* (Luke xv, 31).

L.

JULY 31

What marvel, if I should be wholly set on fire by Thee, and should die to myself; since Thou art a fire always burning and never decaying; a Love purifying the heart and enlightening the understanding.

Bk. IV, ch. xvi.

Remember, Lord, that Thou didst yearn
 To set man's heart aflame
With that consuming fire of love
 Which from Thine own Heart came!
If from a little spark can spring
 A mighty fire, Oh! then
May may heart's love run through the world
 And fire the hearts of men!

P.

AUGUST 1

I will go before thee, and will humble the great ones of the earth (Is. xlv, 2), I will open the gates of the prison, and reveal to thee hidden secrets.

Bk. III, ch. xxiii.

I showed her a picture of St Joan of Arc in prison, comforted by her voices: "I too am comforted by an interior voice," she said, "the Saints encourage me from Heaven, and tell me that as long as I am in fetters I cannot fulfil my mission, but that after my death will begin the time of my conquests."

C.

AUGUST 2

He that hath true and perfect charity seeks himself in no one thing; but desires only the glory of God in all things. He attributes nothing of good to any man, but refers it totally to God, from whom all things proceed as from their fountain; in the enjoyment of whom all the saints repose as in their last end.

Bk. I, ch. xv.

She had been brought a sheaf of corn, and, taking an ear that was so full that the stalk bent under its weight, she looked long at it, and then said to the Prioress:

"This is a figure of my soul, weighed down with graces for myself and for many others. I will always bow down beneath the outpouring of divine grace, knowing that it is the gift of God."

H.

AUGUST 3

The humble man having received reproach, maintains himself well enough in peace, because he is fixed in God, and not in the world. If thou canst but hold thy peace and suffer, thou shalt see without doubt that the Lord will help thee.

Bk. II, ch. ii.

She had been misunderstood, but only remarked gently: "How wise Our Lady was to keep all things in her heart. You cannot blame me for imitating her."

N.V.

AUGUST 4

I must be content with the light of true faith, and walk therein till the day of eternal brightness breaks forth, and the shades of figures pass away.

Bk. IV, ch. xi.

"I have asked Almighty God to send me a beautiful dream to console me for your loss."

"That is a thing I should never have done. To think of your asking for consolations! As you want to resemble me, remember that I say: *Fear not, I shall not waken Thee, O Lord, my soul in peace awaits eternal day.* What a blessed thing it is to serve God in trials and in the night; we have only this life in which to live by faith!"

C.

AUGUST 5

True glory and holy joy is to glory in Thee, and not in one's self; to rejoice in Thy name, and not to be delighted in one's virtue, nor in any creature, save only for Thy sake.

Let Thy name be praised, not mine; let Thy work be extolled, not mine; let Thy holy name be blessed; but to me let nothing be attributed of the praises of men. Thou art my glory; Thou art the joy of my heart.

Bk. III, ch. xl.

Your letter did me so much good, especially the following passage: *Let us keep back any word which would make others think better of us.* We must keep all for Our Lord with jealous care; it is such a joy to work for Him alone . . . My only ambition is Our Lord's glory; as to mine, I leave it to Him. If He seems to forget me, well, He is free to do so, as I no longer belong to myself, but to Him. He will tire of keeping me waiting before I tire of waiting for Him.

L.

AUGUST 6

That good and delightful affection which thou sometimes perceivest, is the effect of present grace, and a certain foretaste of thy heavenly country. But thou must not rely too much upon it, because it goes and comes.

Bk. III, ch. vi.

The divine Shepherd of our souls deprives us of the sense of His presence, that He may bestow consolations on sinners. If He takes us to Thabor, it is only for a few moments, for pastures are usually found in the valley, and it is there that *He rests at midday* (Cant. i, 6).

L.

AUGUST 7

Thy Beloved is of such a nature that He will admit of no other; but will have thy heart to Himself, and sit there like a king on His own throne.

Bk. II, ch. vii.

Lo, I am Thy servant, ready to obey Thee in all things; for I do not desire to live for myself, but for Thee; O that I could do so after a faithful and perfect manner!

Bk. III, ch. xv.

Now that I am about to appear before God, I understand very clearly that one thing only is necessary: to work for Him alone, and not for oneself or for others. Our Lord wants to take sole possession of your heart; this can only be at the price of much suffering . . . but what joy will be yours when you enter Heaven! . . . I am not dying, I am entering into life, and what I cannot explain on earth I will make known to you from Heaven.

L.

AUGUST 8

When thou hast Christ thou art rich, and He is sufficient for thee; He will provide for thee, and will be thy faithful Procurator in all things, so that thou needst not trust to men. For men quickly change and presently fail: but Christ remains for ever, and stands by us firmly to the end.

Bk. II, ch. i.

We can lean on nothing but Our Lord, for He alone is immutable. What joy to know that He can never change!

L.

AUGUST 9

Wherefore, O Lord God, I take it for a great benefit not to have much which, outwardly and according to men, might appear praiseworthy and glorious; so that a person, considering his own poverty and meanness, ought not upon that account to be weighed down, or to be grieved and dejected, but rather to receive comfort and great pleasure. Because Thou, O God, hast chosen the poor and the humble, and those that are despised by this world, for Thy familiar friends and domestics.

Bk. III, ch. xxii.

She frequently had her side cauterized, and one day after a painful treatment was resting during recreation, when she overheard the following remark being made in the kitchen: "Sœur Thérèse will soon die, but I wonder what Mother Prioress will find to say about her when she is gone. It will not be an easy task, because, although so pleasant and amiable, she has never done anything worth talking about."

The infirmarian also overheard these words, and remarked to the Saint: "What a good thing you never relied on the opinion of others, you would be bitterly disappointed today!" she replied: "Thank God I have always had the grace to feel indifferent to what others thought of me."

H.

AUGUST 10

The holy martyr Laurence overcame the world, with his prelate; because he despised whatever seemed delightful in this world; and for the love of Christ he also suffered the high priest of God, Sixtus, whom he exceedingly loved, to be taken away from him. He overcame, therefore, the love of man by the love of the Creator: and instead of the comfort he had in man, he made choice rather of God's pleasure.

So do thou also learn to part with a necessary and beloved friend for the love of God.

Bk. II, ch. ix.

I had a great longing to see Céline a nun at the Carmel of Lisieux, but this hope seemed beyond the bounds of possibility. I sacrificed my wish, committing my beloved sister's future entirely to God, content to see her go, if necessary, to the other side of the world, if only she might be, like myself, a bride of Christ. I suffered so much at seeing her exposed in the world to dangers of which I had known nothing. I felt such affectionate solicitude for her soul, that my sisterly love was more like that of a mother.

H.

AUGUST 11

God regards more with how much affection and love a person performs a work, than how much he does.

Bk. I, ch. xv.

> The daily work, that claims thy care,
>   Thy heart must still leave free
> To do a nobler work by far:
> Love's craftsman thou must be!
> In mocking eyes, thy empty hands
>   Can claim no meed of praise;
> Love labours, all unseen by men,
>   A perfect work to raise.

P.

AUGUST 12

Jesus Christ alone is singularly to be loved, who alone is found good and faithful above all friends.

Bk. II, ch. viii.

He who is so soon to become my Bridegroom has been
infinitely loving and merciful in not allowing me to
become attached to anything here below. He knows
that if I had found the slightest source of happiness,
I would have clung to it with all my strength, so He has
denied me the least trace of happiness. Rather than
allow me to follow a light which was not His light, He
has kept me in darkness, I do not want creatures to
have any of my love, I want to keep it all for Jesus, as
true happiness can only be found in Him. All shall be
for Him, all; and when I have nothing to give, as is
the case this evening, I will give Him that nothing.

L.

AUGUST 13

Behold, if all should be said against thee which the
malice of men can invent, what hurt could it do thee, if
thou wouldst let it pass, and make no account of it?
Could it even so much as pluck one hair from thee?

But he who has not his heart within, nor God before
his eyes, is easily moved with a word of dispraise.
Whereas he that trusts in Me, and desires not to stand
by his own judgement, will be free from the fear of
men. For I am the judge and discerner of all secrets; I
know how matters are; I know him that offers the injury and him that suffers it. From Me this word went
forth; by My permission it happened; *that out of many
hearts thoughts may be revealed* (Luke ii, 35).

Bk. III, ch. xlvi.

"When I am corrected," I said to her one day, "I
prefer to have deserved it, rather than be unjustly
accused."

"I would rather be unjustly reproved," she answered,
"because having a good conscience I can then offer it

joyfully to God; but afterwards I humble myself with the thought that I am quite capable of committing the fault in question. As you advance in the spiritual life you will not have to struggle so much, or rather, you will overcome difficulties more easily, as you will approach them in the right way. Your soul will have been lifted above creatures. I no longer care what is said to me, because I know how faulty human judgement can be, What is the use of justifying ourselves when we are misunderstood or misjudged? Say nothing, let the matter drop, one can even rejoice in being misjudged. The Gospel does not say that St Mary Magdalen defended herself, when accused by her sister of neglecting her duty as she sat at Our Lord's feet. She did not say: "Oh! Martha, if you only knew what happiness there is in listening to the words of the Master, you too would leave all to share in my joy and rest!" St Mary Magdalen, however, preferred to say nothing . . . O blessed silence, that brings such peace to the soul."

C.

AUGUST 14

It is a very great thing to stand in obedience, to live under a superior, and not to be at our own disposal. It is much more secure to be in the state of subjection, than authority.

Many are under obedience more out of necessity than for the love of God; and such as these are in pain, and easily repine. Nor will they gain freedom of mind, unless they submit themselves with their whole heart for God's sake.

Bk. I, ch. ix.

Dear Mother, you are the compass Jesus has given me, by which to reach the shores of eternity. I look at you, and then do Our Lord's will. Whilst allowing me to undergo temptations against faith, the divine Master has greatly increased the spirit of faith in my soul, by which I see Him living in you, and giving me His commands through you. I know that you make the burden of obedience sweet and easy, but I am convinced that if you began to treat me with severity, I should not change my attitude towards you, nor would my filial affection grow less, because I should still see God's will expressed in another way for the greater good of my soul.

H.

AUGUST 15

They are filled with so great a love of the Deity, and such overflowing joy, that there is nothing wanting to their glory, nor can any happiness be wanting to them. All the saints, by how much the higher they are in glory, by so much are they the more humble in themselves, and nearer to Me, and better beloved by Me.

Bk. III, ch. lviii.

It is true that Our Lady is Queen of Heaven and earth, but at the same time she is more Mother than Queen. One should not think of her (as I have often heard it said) eclipsing the glory of all the Saints, as the rising sun makes the stars disappear. That would be a very strange thing, for a mother to overshadow the glory of her children. On the contrary, I believe that she will add splendour to the glory of the Saints.

N.V.

AUGUST 16

Why dost thou stand looking about thee here, since this is not thy resting place? Let thy thoughts be with the Most High, and thy prayer directed to Christ without intermission.

Bk. II, ch. i.

The Saint obeyed the Rule, and never looked about her in the refectory. As I found difficulty in being faithful on this point, she composed a prayer which was a revelation of her humility, for in it she asked for a grace which only I needed: "O Jesus, Thy two little brides have resolved never to look up in the refectory, in order to honour and imitate the example Thou didst give them before Herod. When that wicked prince mocked Thee, O Infinite Beauty, Thou didst utter no word of complaint, nor even look at him. Herod did not deserve a look from Thy divine eyes, but we, Thy brides, desire it. Reward us with a look of love each time we make the sacrifice of not looking up, and do the same even if we fail in our resolution, for we will then humble ourselves sincerely in Thy sight."

C.

August 17

Let curiosities alone. Read such matters as may rather move thee to compunction, than give thee occupation.

Bk. I, ch. xx.

A novice had brought her, by way of recreation, an entertaining book full of illustrations, but the Saint refused it, saying: "How could you think that such a book would interest me! I am too near eternity to be distracted with trifles."

N.V.

August 18

Vanity of vanities, and all is vanity, besides loving God

and serving Him alone. This is the highest wisdom:
by despising the world to tend to heavenly kingdoms.

It is vanity to mind only this present life, and not to
look forward to those things which are to come. It is
vanity to love that which passeth with all speed, and not
to hasten thither where everlasting joy remains. Often
remember that proverb: *The eye is not satisfied with
seeing, nor is the ear filled with hearing* (Eccles. i, 8).

Bk. I, ch. i.

Jesus, hidden in my poor little heart, has once again
made me understand how hollow and empty are all
passing things. To the astonishment of the Community
I have been able to paint a little, write poetry, and do
some good to souls. Just as Solomon said: *I turned
myself to all the works which my hands had wrought, and
to the labours wherein I had laboured in vain, I saw in all
things vanity and vexation of mind, and that nothing was
lasting under the sun* (Eccles. ii, 2), so have I learned by
experience that there is no happiness on earth save in
hiding oneself and remaining in ignorance of all created
things. Without love, even the greatest works are as
nothing. Instead of wounding my soul and doing me
harm, God's gifts draw me closer to Him, for I see that
He alone is unchanging and can satisfy my immense
desires.

H.

AUGUST 19

Lord, I stand much in need of a grace yet greater, if
I must arrive so far that it may not be in the power of
any man or anything created to hinder me. For as long
as anything holds me, I cannot freely fly to Thee. He
was desirous to fly freely to Thee, who said: *Who will*

give me wings like a dove, and I will fly away and be at rest
(Ps. liv, 7).

What can be more at rest than a simple eye that aims
at nothing but God? And what can be more free than
he who desires nothing upon earth? A man ought therefore to pass and ascend above everything created, and
perfectly to forsake himself, and in ecstasy of mind to
stand and see that no creatures can be compared with
Thee; because Thou infinitely transcendest them all.

Bk. III, ch. xxxi.

Thank God I have never met with anything but dis-
appointment in human friendships. A heart like mine
would have been taken captive and its wings clipped,
and then I could no longer *fly away and be at rest*. How
can a heart given up to human love ever be intimately
united to God? It is impossible. I have seen so many
souls, attracted by its false light, burn their wings like
hapless moths, and then come back wounded to Jesus,
the divine Fire which burns and consumes not.

H.

AUGUST 20

No man hath so lively a feeling of the Passion of
Christ, as he who hath happened to suffer like things.

Bk. II, ch. ii.

The charity of Christ is never diminished, and the
greatness of His propitiation is never exhausted.

Bk. IV, ch. ii.

One Sunday, as I closed my missal after Mass, a
picture of the Crucifixion slipped out a little beyond
the pages, only one pierced hand showing. I was filled

with a strange emotion I had never felt before. The sight of the Precious Blood running down unheeded, no one troubling to gather it up, broke my heart. I resolved always to remain in spirit at the foot of the Cross, to receive the heavenly dew of salvation and give it to souls.

Christ's dying cry: *I thirst!* re-echoed in my heart, and increased my burning love. I longed to give Him to drink, and was myself tortured with a thirst for souls, and a desire to save them from perdition.

H.

AUGUST 21

Nature doth all for her own lucre and interest; she can do nothing gratis, but hopes to gain something equal or better, or praise, or favour for her good deeds; and covets to have her actions and gifts much valued. But grace seeks nothing temporal, nor requires any other recompense but God alone for her reward, nor desires anything more of the necessaries of this life than may be serviceable for the obtaining a happy eternity.

Bk. III, ch. liv.

If a man take away thy coat, let go thy cloak also unto him (Matt. v, 40). To let go one's cloak must surely mean to give up all rights, to consider oneself the servant and slave of others. It is easier to walk or run without a cloak, so Jesus adds: *Whosoever will force thee one mile, go with him other two* (ibid., 41). It is not enough to give what is asked of me, I must foresee another's need, show that she does me an honour by asking a service of me; and if anything is taken from me, appear glad to be rid of it.

It is not always possible to obey this passage from the Gospel literally; sometimes I am obliged to refuse.

But where charity has taken deep root in a soul, it shows outwardly: a refusal may be so gracious that it gives as much pleasure as a gift. An obliging person is, of course, being made use of continually, but that is no reason for avoiding those whom one might have to refuse, for Our Lord says: *From him that would borrow of thee, turn not away* (ibid., 42). Nor must I be obliging merely to appear so, or in the hope of getting some little service in return, for Our Lord has said: *If you lend to them of whom you hope to receive, what thanks are to you? for sinners also lend to sinners, for to receive as much. Do good, and lend, hoping for nothing thereby: and your reward shall be great* (Luke vi, 34, 35).

H.

AUGUST 22

In regard to that little of thy will which thou now willingly forsakest, thou shalt for ever have thy will in heaven. For there thou shalt find all that thou willest, all that thou canst desire.

There thou shalt enjoy all good, without fear of ever losing it. There thy will, being always one with mine, shall desire nothing foreign or private.

Bk. III, ch. xlix.

God will do my will in Heaven, because I never did it on earth.

C.

AUGUST 23

O most happy mansion of the city above! O most bright day of eternity, which knows no night, but is always enlightened by the Sovereign Truth! a day always joyful, always secure, and never changing its

state for the contrary! O that this day would shine
upon us, and all those temporal things come to an end!

Bk. III, ch. xlviii.

Although big feasts did not often occur, there was one,
very dear to me, that each week brought round—Sunday. It was the day of rest, God's own feast-day. The
happy day was over all too soon, and so was tinged with
melancholy. Until Compline my happiness was complete, but as soon as the evening office had been said,
my heart grew sad. I thought of the morrow, when
ordinary life would begin again, with work to be done
and lessons to be learnt. This world seemed a land of
exile and I longed for eternal rest, for the Sunday which
would have no sunset in our own true home-land.

H.

AUGUST 24

The reason why we are so willing to talk is because by
discoursing together we seek comfort from one another,
and would gladly ease the heart, wearied by various
thoughts. And we very willingly talk and think of such
things as we most love and desire, or which we imagine
contrary to us. But, alas! it is often in vain and to no
purpose: for this outward consolation is no small
hindrance of interior and divine comfort.

Bk. I, ch. x.

I had asked her advice on several matters, and she
said: "If we refrain from seeking relief by talking about
our own troubles, God gives us the grace to guide and
comfort other souls. By acting otherwise we do not find
relief, but only aggravate the trouble."

N.V.

AUGUST 25

Desires often inflame thee, and violently hurry thee
on; but consider whether it be for My honour or thy
own interest that thou art more moved. If thou hast
no other view but Me, thou wilt be well contented with
whatever I shall ordain: for if there lurk in thee anything of self-seeking, behold this it is that hinders thee
and troubles thee.

Take care then not to rely too much upon any desire
which thou hast conceived before thou hast consulted
Me, lest afterwards thou repent, or be displeased with
that which before pleased thee, and which thou zealously
didst desire as the best. For every inclination which
appears good is not presently to be followed: nor every
contrary affection at first sight to be rejected.

Even in good desires and inclinations, it is expedient
sometimes to use some restraint; lest by too much
eagerness thou incur distraction of mind; lest thou
create scandal to others by not keeping within discipline,
or by the opposition which thou mayest meet with from
others, thou be suddenly disturbed and fall.

Bk. III, ch. xi.

She warned me that when it became known after her
death that she had been the spiritual sister of two
missionaries, many young priests would ask for a like
favour, but that it might be dangerous for certain souls:
"Anyone could write what I write, and would receive
the same compliments and inspire the same confidence;
but we can be of use to the Church by prayer and
sacrifice. Such correspondences should be allowed
rarely, and denied altogether to those nuns who would
think too much about it. They would imagine they
were doing wonders, whereas they would only be harm-

ing their own souls, and might be deceived by the wiles of the devil.

Do not forget what I say as time goes on, for it is most important. We must not mint false coin at Carmel with which to buy souls. How often the fine letters one writes, and that one receives in return, are nothing more than an exchange of worthless coin."

N.V.

AUGUST 26

Turn thine eyes back upon thyself, and see thou judge not the doings of others. In judging others a man labours in vain, often errs, and easily sins: but in judging and in looking into himself, he always labours with fruit.

Bk. I, ch. xiv.

He that judges me is the Lord; Jesus Christ is my judge. In order to obtain a favourable verdict, or rather, to escape being judged at all, for He has said: *Judge not and you shall not be judged* (Luke vi, 37), I shall try always to have charitable thoughts.

H.

AUGUST 27

Why wilt thou put off thy resolutions from day to day? Arise, and begin this very moment, and say: Now is the time for doing and now is the time to fight; now is the proper time to amend my life.

Bk. I, ch. xxii.

Marie had taken Pauline's place; every evening I listened eagerly to the beautiful things she told me. Her great and generous heart seemed to pass into mine. As

warriors of olden times taught their children the use
of arms, so she taught me how to fight life's battle,
arousing my enthusiasm and showing me the path of
victory. She spoke of the spiritual riches it is so easy
to amass day by day, and how foolish it would be to
trample them underfoot, when one only has to stoop
and pick them up.

H.

AUGUST 28

Be mindful of the resolution thou hast taken, and set
before thee the image of the Crucified. Well mayest
thou be ashamed, if thou hast looked upon the life of
Jesus Christ, that thou hast not yet studied to conform
thyself more to His pattern, although thou hast been
long in the way of God.

Bk. I, ch. xxv.

Why seekest thou rest, since thou art born to labour?
Dispose thyself to patience, rather than consolation;
and to bear the cross, rather than to rejoice.

Bk. II, ch. x.

I saw religious life as it really is, with all its restraints,
and the little daily sacrifices that others do not suspect.
I realized how easy it would be to become wrapped up
in oneself, and to forget the sublime end of our vocation,
so I said to myself: Later on, when trials come, and I
am a prisoner at Carmel where I can only see a little
corner of blue sky, I shall remember today, and the
memory of this beautiful scenery will encourage me.
I shall forget my own petty interests as I think of
God's majesty and power: I shall love Him alone,
and not become attached to trifles, for I have had as

it were a glimpse of what is prepared for those that love Him.

H.

August 29

If it be deferred, let us believe that we are not well prepared, and that we are as yet unworthy of the great glory which shall be revealed in us at the appointed time; and let us endeavour to prepare ourselves better for our departure. *Blessed is that servant, whom when his lord shall come, he shall find watching. Amen I say to you, he shall set him over all his possessions* (Luke xii, 43).

Bk. I, ch. xix.

I know that I shall die soon, but the day of my death is always being postponed. I am like a child who has been promised a cake; every time he stretches out his hand for it, it is withdrawn out of reach. I am quite resigned to live or to die, I am even willing to recover and go to Cochin-China if it is God's will.

N.V.

August 30

God would have thee learn to suffer tribulation without comfort, and wholly to submit thyself to Him, and to become more humble by tribulation.

Bk. II, ch. xii.

There are some who take such a gloomy view of things that they make them much worse; I always look on the bright side. If I have suffering unrelieved by any gleam of comfort, I manage to make that my joy.

C.

AUGUST 31

Then the flesh that has been mortified shall triumph more than if it had always been pampered in delights. Then will a strict life and a hard penance be more pleasing than all the delights of the earth.

Bk. I, ch. xxiv.

After having, like Jesus Christ, passed through this life doing good; after having been overlooked, misunderstood, as He was, the Saint was to scale a hard and painful Calvary. As the Prioress was used to seeing her carry on bravely in spite of illness, she allowed her to keep the observance, although she found some of the Community exercises very tiring. At the end of the day, when she went upstairs unaided, she had to wait at every step to take breath, and reached her cell so exhausted that she sometimes took an hour to undress. When at length she went to bed, it was on a hard straw mattress that she took her brief rest.

She passed very bad nights, but when asked if she did not need some attention, she answered: "Oh! no, I am glad to have a cell at some distance from the others, as they cannot hear me. I prefer to suffer alone; as soon as I am petted, I no longer *enjoy myself.*"

H.

SEPTEMBER 1

(Christ.) Son, thou hast many things still to learn, which thou hast not yet well learned.

(Disciple.) What are these things, O Lord?

(Christ.) That thou conform in all things thy desire to My good pleasure; and that thou be not a lover of thyself, but earnestly zealous that My will may be done. Desires often inflame thee, and violently hurry thee on;

but consider whether it be for My honour or thy own interest that thou art more moved.

Bk. III, ch. xi.

My year of novitiate, which had seemed so long, at last came to an end, but Mother Prioress told me that my Profession was out of the question, as our ecclesiastical Superior would not allow it. I was obliged, therefore, to wait for another eight months.

At first I found it hard to make the sacrifice, but soon God enlightened my soul. I was meditating at the time on P. Surin's *Foundations of the Spiritual Life*. One day during prayer I understood how much self-love there was in my longing to make my vows. If I belonged to Jesus as His little plaything, to rejoice and comfort Him, I ought not to force Him to do my will instead of His own. I also understood that a bride should be adorned with jewels on her wedding day, and I had not thought of this. I therefore said to Our Lord: I will no longer ask to make my Profession; I am content to wait, but I do not want our union to be put off through my fault, so I will pre are a bridal dress resplendent with diamonds and precious stones. When it is rich enough, Thou wilt take me for Thy bride.

H.

September 2

O most blessed grace, which makest the poor in spirit rich in virtues, and renderest him who is rich in many good things, humble of heart.

Bk. III, ch. lv.

"What do you think of the many graces which have been showered on you?"

"I think that *the Spirit breatheth where he will*"
(John iii, 8).

C.

SEPTEMBER 3

Thou must be content to be made a fool for Christ,
if thou wilt lead a religious life.

Bk. I, ch. xvii.

I am very glad, Céline, that you do not feel any
natural attraction for Carmel now that you are about to
enter; this is a delicate attention on the part of Our
Lord who is enabling you to make Him a gift. He
knows that it is more blessed to give than to receive.
How blessed also to suffer reproach for the sake of Him
who loves us, and to pass for fools in the eyes of the
world! The foolish world, judging us by its own standard, calls us by this name, but let us take comfort in the
thought that we are not the first. The only crime of
which Herod accused Our Lord was madness . . . and
in a sense he was right. It was indeed madness for the
King of Glory, seated above the Cherubim, to seek out
poor human hearts in which to set up His throne. Was
He not infinitely happy with the Father and the Spirit
of Love? Why come down on earth to make sinners
His intimate friends?

We could never go to such lengths of folly to repay
our Bridegroom; compared with His, our actions are
quite reasonable. Let the world then leave us in peace,
for it is the world which is foolish, knowing nothing of
all Jesus has done and suffered to save it from perdition.

L.

SEPTEMBER 4

Temptations are often very profitable to a man,

although they be troublesome and grievous: for in them a man is humbled, purified, and instructed. All the saints have passed through many tribulations and have profited by them: and they who could not support temptations have become reprobate, and fell off.

There is not any Order so holy, nor place so retired, where there are not temptations and adversities.

Bk. I, ch. xiii.

On the eve of Profession—which is usually spent in holy joy and peace before the dawn of the great day— I suddenly saw my vocation as a delusion, a dream. The devil—for it was assuredly he—inspired me with the conviction that the life of a Carmelite was quite unsuited to me, and that I was deceiving my Superiors by continuing in it in spite of having no vocation. I was plunged into such darkness that I could only see one thing clearly, which was, that not being called to the religious life, I must go back to the world. My distress was indescribable and I did not know what to do. However, I did the very best thing by revealing this temptation to my novice mistress; I called her out of choir, and feeling much ashamed told her in what state I was. Luckily she saw through the temptation, and laughingly reassured me.

My act of humility instantly put the devil to flight; he had tried to make me conceal the trial and so fall into the trap, but he himself was caught, for I told all to Mother Prioress as well, and her consoling answer dispelled any lingering doubts.

H.

SEPTEMBER 5

Never promise thyself security in this life, though thou seemest to be a good religious, or a devout hermit.

Oftentimes, they that were better in the judgement of men, have been in greater danger by reason of their too great confidence. So that it is better for many not to be altogether free from temptations, but to be often assaulted, that they may not be too secure; lest perhaps they be lifted up with pride, or take more liberty to go aside after exterior comforts.

Bk. I, ch. xx.

"I know that if I gave way deliberately to the least infidelity, my mind would become so darkened that I could no longer accept death."

As the Prioress showed surprise at these words, she added: "I am speaking of a sin of pride. If, for instance, I were to say: "I have acquired such or such a virtue and can practise it," or, "My God, I love Thee too much ever to entertain for a moment a thought against faith!" I feel that I should at once be assailed by such terrible temptations that I should give way. To avoid such a disaster, I have only to say humbly with my whole heart: "My God, I beseech of Thee, let me not be unfaithful!"

C.

SEPTEMBER 6

The lover looks not at the gifts, but turns himself to the Giver, above all goods.

Bk. III, ch. v.

One day she was throwing rose-petals up at the crucifix in the garth. "Are you hoping to obtain some grace?" we asked her.

"Oh! no," was her quick reply, "it is to please Our Lord. I do not give in order to receive."

E.

SEPTEMBER 7

Delight in the Lord and he will give thee the requests of thy heart (Ps. xxxvi, 4). For if thou wilt be delighted in truth, and receive more abundant consolation from Me, behold, in the contempt of all worldly things, and in the renouncing of all those mean pleasures, thou shalt be blessed, and an exceeding great comfort be derived to thy soul. And the more thou withdrawest thyself from all comfort in things created, the more sweet and the more powerful consolations wilt thou find in Me.

Bk. III, ch. xii.

St Teresa had care of the statue of the Child Jesus in the cloister. On the eve of her Profession, Sœur Marie du Sacré-Cœur noticed with surprise that she had arranged the same candles which had burnt on her Clothing day, instead of the new pink ones provided. The Saint sent her the following note in explanation: "The others mean far more to me. They looked so fresh and pink on my Clothing day; my Father had given them, and he was present, and all was joy. Now their colour has faded. Are these any rose-coloured joys for your little Teresa to be found on earth? No, there is nothing left but heavenly joys; created things, which are empty and vain, have given place to the great reality, which is uncreated."

L.

SEPTEMBER 8

Let My promise strengthen thee and comfort thee in all events. Peace shall come in one day, which is known to the Lord: and it shall not be a vicissitude of day and night, such as is at present; but everlasting light, infinite brightness, steadfast peace, and secure rest. For death shall be no more, but never-failing health: no anxiety, but blessed delight, and a society sweet and lovely.

Lift up therefore thy face to heaven.

Bk. III, ch. xlvii.

Our Lady's birthday! What a beautiful feast on which to become the bride of Christ, baby Mary a day old presenting His little flower to little Jesus! On that day everything was little except the graces I received ,and the peace and joy I felt when evening came and I gazed up at the starry heavens, where I would soon be united to my divine Bridegroom in everlasting happiness.

From the time I awoke in the morning I was filled with peace, and it was in *the peace of God which surpasseth all understanding* (Phil. iv, 7) that I pronounced my holy vows. At the close of this beautiful day I laid my wreath, as is the custom, at Our Lady's feet without any feeling of sadness, for I felt that time would not lessen my happiness.

O Jesus, I only ask Thee to give me peace! . . . Peace, and above all a love that knews no bounds.

H.

SEPTEMBER 9

The world promises things temporal and of small value, and is served with great eagerness; I promise things most excellent and everlasting, and men's hearts are not moved! *Be thou ashamed, O Sidon,* saith the sea.

Alas! for an unchangeable good, for an inestimable reward, for the highest honours and never-ending glory, they are unwilling to take the least pains. Be ashamed, then, thou slothful servant!

Bk. III, ch. iii.

A week after I received the veil, our cousin Jeanne
Guérin was married to Dr. La Néele. When she next
came to the parlour and spoke of the affectionate consideration she showed her husband, my heart was
moved, and I thought: It shall not be said that a woman
of the world does more for her husband, a mere mortal,
than I do for my beloved Lord!

I was filled with fresh fervour, and tried more than
ever in all I did to please my heavenly Bridegroom, the
King of kings, who has deigned to make me His bride.

H.

SEPTEMBER 10

Man's merits are not to be estimated by his having
many visions or consolations, nor by his knowledge of
Scriptures, nor by his being placed in a more elevated
station; but by his being grounded in true humility,
and replenished with divine charity; by his seeking
always, purely and entirely, the honour of God; by his
esteeming himself as nothing, and sincerely despising
himself; and being better pleased to be despised and
humbled by others, than to be the object of their
esteem.

Bk. III, ch. vii.

Amongst those of the Community who came into
contact with the Saint during her last illness was a laysister who could not understand her reputation for
sanctity, as she had only seen her carrying out faithfully
very ordinary duties. One day she brought the dying
nun some food which would certainly have made her
sick, so it was gently refused with an apology. The
Sister was displeased, and remarked later: "I cannot
understand why Sœur Thérèse is so much praised;

she never does anything out of the ordinary; in fact, she could scarcely be called a good religious."

When this was repeated to the Saint, her face lit up with a smile, and she told a nun who came to see her how happy it made her to be so judged: "What joy to hear on my death-bed that I am not even a good nun!

Sum.

SEPTEMBER 11

A priest, clad in his sacred vestments, is Christ's viceregent to pray to God for himself and for all the people, in a suppliant and humble manner.

He has before him and behind him the sign of the Cross of the Lord, that he may always remember the Passion of Christ. He bears the cross before him in his vestment, that he may diligently behold the footsteps of Christ, and fervently endeavour to follow them. He is marked with a cross behind, that he may mildly suffer, for God's sake, whatsoever adversities shall befall him from others. He wears the cross before him, that he may bewail his own sins; and behind him, that through compassion he may lament the sins of others, and know that he is placed, as it were, a mediator betwixt God and the sinner. Neither ought he to cease from prayer and the holy oblation, till he be favoured with the grace and mercy which he implores.

Bk. IV, ch. v.

The harvest-time had not yet come,
But Thou didst yearn to see
The golden grain all garnered safe
In Heaven's granary.
Lord of the harvest, send Thy priests
To reap where Thou didst sow!
To them I dedicate my life,
My sufferings here below.

P.

SEPTEMBER 12

Conceive an indignation against thyself; suffer not the swelling of pride to live in thee; but make thyself so submissive and little, that all may trample on thee, and tread thee under their feet, as the dust of the streets.

Bk. III, ch. xiii.

Grant that I may keep my vows in all their perfection, that no one may notice me, that I may be trodden underfoot and forgotten as a grain of sand. I offer myself to Thee, my well-Beloved, that Thy holy will may be fulfilled in me, without let or hindrance on the part of creatures.

H.

SEPTEMBER 13

He does much that does well what he does.

Bk. I, ch. xv.

Union with God was the chief theme of her instructions to the novices. She would reprove one for idly humming an air, another for carelessly sitting sideways on her chair, saying sadly: "How few there are who do everything as well as they can! The majority are content with half measures and careless ways".

E.

SEPTEMBER 14

Lord Jesus, I have received the cross, I have received it from Thy hand: and I will bear it until death, as Thou hast laid it upon me. Indeed the life of a good religious man is a cross, but it is a cross that conducts him to Paradise.

Bk. III, ch. lvi.

Instead of reproaching Our Lord for having sent us this cross, I cannot fathom the depths of divine love which move Him so to treat us. God must love Father very dearly to send him such suffering. What joy for us to share this humiliation with him!

L.

SEPTEMBER 15

Drink of the chalice of thy Lord lovingly, if thou desirest to be His friend, and to have part with Him.

Bk. II, ch. xii.

During her long agony which lasted twelve hours, she cried out: "O my God, O sweet Virgin Mary, come to my help! My chalice is overflowing; I could not have thought it possible to suffer so much . . . I can only explain it by my great longing to save souls. O my God, Thy will be done, only have pity on me!"

H.

SEPTEMBER 16

Help me, O Lord God, in my good resolution, and in Thy holy service, and give me grace now, this day, perfectly to begin, for what I hitherto have done is nothing.

According as our resolution is, will the progress of our advancement be: and he hath need of much diligence who would advance much. Let us endeavour what we can, we shall still be apt to fail in many things.

Bk. I, ch. xix.

If a man does what lies in him, and is truly penitent, as often as he shall come to Me for pardon and grace, as I live, saith the Lord, I will no longer remember his sins, but all shall be forgiven him.

Bk. IV, ch. vii.

I quite agree with you that the many imperfections of His friends wound the Sacred Heart of Jesus more deeply than do the grave faults of His enemies. But, my dear brother, it seems to me that it is only when these failings spring from habit, and are not regretted, that He can say: "What are these wounds in the midst of my hands?" *With these was I wounded in the house of them that loved me* (Zach. xiii, 6). But those who love Him, and who throw themselves into His arms after every fall asking for pardon, only fill His Heart with a new joy.

L.

SEPTEMBER 17

Men's sentiments are often wrong in their judgements; and the lovers of the world are deceived in loving visible things alone.

What is a man the better for being reputed greater by man? One deceitful man deceiveth another; the vain deceives the vain, the blind deceives the blind, the weak the weak, whilst he extols him; and in truth doth rather confound him, whilst he vainly praiseth him.

For how much each one is in Thy eyes, so much he is, and no more, saith the humble St Francis.

Bk. III, ch. I.

To a young Sister, who said that she must be a privileged soul for God to confide other souls to her care, she replied: "I am what I am in God's sight, and nothing more. Because He has made me His interpreter, it does not mean that He has a special love for me, but rather that He has made me your servant. It is for your sake, not mine, that He has given me a certain attractiveness and the virtues that you see in me.

The most privileged souls are those whom God keeps

for Himself alone. As for those who are brought forward, a miracle of grace is needed to preserve their freshness."

E.

SEPTEMBER 18

Behold, the cross is all, and in dying to thyself all consists: and there is no other way to life and true internal peace, but the way of the holy cross and of daily mortification.

Bk. II, ch. xii.

She contrived to hide her mortification under a gracious manner, but I saw her sprinkling wormwood on an extra dish ordered for her by Mother Prioress on a fast-day, and which she found too agreeable to her taste.

Another time I saw her slowly sipping a particularly nasty medicine. "Drink it down quickly!" I urged. "Oh, no!" she replied, "I must take advantage of these little opportunities of mortifying myself, as greater penances are denied me."

H.

SEPTEMBER 19

Oh! how great thanks am I obliged to return to Thee, for having vouchsafed to show me and all the faithful a right and good way to an everlasting kingdom. For Thy life is our way: and by holy patience we walk on to Thee, who art our crown.

If Thou hadst not gone before and instructed us, who would have cared to have followed? Alas! how many would have stayed afar off, and a great way behind, if they had not before their eyes Thy excellent example!

Bk. III, ch. xviii.

I must explain what *the odour of Thy ointments* means to me. As Our Lord has ascended into Heaven, I can only follow His footprints. How fragrant and full of light are the traces He has left on earth! I have only to open the Gospels and at once I find the *most sweet odour* of His life, and know whither to run: not to the first place, but to the last.

H.

SEPTEMBER 20

Lo! thou art made a priest, and art consecrated to say Mass: see now that in due time thou faithfully and devoutly offer up sacrifice to God, and that thou behave thyself in such manner as to be without reproof. Thou hast not lightened thy burden, but art now bound with a stricter bond of discipline, and art obliged to a greater perfection of sanctity.

Bk. IV, ch. v.

The sanctification of priests held the first place in her apostolic zeal. She writes to her sister: "Do not let us waste the short time that remains, let us save souls! I feel that Jesus wants us to slake His thirst by giving Him souls, above all the souls of priests. So let us consecrate our lives to them and pray much for priests. Their souls should be clear as crystal, but alas, many are not what they ought to be. Let us then pray and suffer for them; I know you understand my soul's longing."

The Saint was only sixteen when she wrote these lines.

L.

SEPTEMBER 21

For the profit of one that stands in need, a good work is sometimes freely to be omitted, or rather to be changed for a better. For by doing thus, a good work is not lost, but is changed into a better.

Bk. I, ch. xv.

"When the bell rings for us, or someone knocks, we must mortify ourselves and not do another stitch before answering. I have practised this, and can assure you that it is a source of peace to the soul."

After the Saint had given me this advice I followed it faithfully. One day during her last illness she witnessed my prompt obedience: "When you come to die," she said, "you will rejoice to see your merit. You have done a more glorious thing than if you had been clever enough to win the goodwill of the Government towards religious communities, and all France acclaimed you a Judith."

C.

SEPTEMBER 22

We have now begun; it is not lawful to go back, nor may we leave off. Take courage, my brethren; let us go forward together; Jesus will be with us. For the sake of Jesus we took up His cross, and for His sake let us persevere in it. He will be our helper, who is our captain and our leader. Behold, our King marches before us, who will fight for us!

Bk. III, ch. lvi.

Lord God of armies, who hast said: *I came not to bring peace but the sword* (Matt. x, 34), arm me for the combat! I am all on fire to fight for Thy glory, but give me courage, so that I may say like David: *Blessed be the Lord my God, who teacheth my hands to fight, and my fingers to war* (Ps. cxliii, 1).

My Beloved, I know well where Thou wouldst have me to fight, and that it is not upon a battle-field. My sword is Love, and with it I must drive out the stranger from the land, and establish Thy kingdom in souls. O Jesus, I will wield my sword in this cause all the days of my life!

Pr.

SEPTEMBER 23

If thou hadst once perfectly entered into the interior of Jesus, and experienced a little of His burning love, then wouldst thou not care at all for thy own convenience or inconvenience, but wouldst rather rejoice at reproach; because the love of Jesus makes a man despise himself.

Bk. II, ch. i.

Instead of avoiding humiliations she sought them eagerly, and for this reason offered to work with a nun who was notoriously hard to please, her generous offer being accepted. One day when she had been well scolded, a novice asked her why she looked so happy. She was much surprised to get the following answer: "It is because Sister N. has been saying some very unpleasant things to me, and I am so glad. I only wish I could meet her, so as to give her a smile."

At that moment the Sister in question knocked at the door, and the wondering novice was able to see how the Saints forgive.

"My soul moved so far above such things," the Saint said later, "that humiliations were actually a source of strength to me."

H.

SEPTEMBER 24

I am poor and in labours from my youth: and my soul is grieved even unto tears sometimes. Thou alone art true joy, Thou my hope and my crown, Thou my gladness and my honour, O Lord!

Bk. III, ch. 1.

Thou impartest unto them much consolation, to support them in their many troubles; and Thou liftest them up from the depth of their own dejection, to the hope of Thy protection; and Thou dost re-create and enlighten them interiorly with a new grace.

Thou art pleased to deal thus with Thy elect, to the end that they may truly acknowledge and plainly experience how great is their infirmity when left to themselves, and how much they receive from Thy bounty and grace.

Bk. IV, ch. iv.

I received the veil on September 24, a day all veiled in tears. My father was too ill to come and bless his queen; at the last moment Mgr Hugonin was prevented from performing the ceremony, and several circumstances combined to make it a sad and depressing day. Yet there was peace in my cup of sorrow. Our Lord willed that I should not be able to keep back my tears . . . and they were misunderstood. I had been through much greater trials before, dry-eyed, with the help of grace, but this time I was left to my own resources, and proved how weak they were.

H.

SEPTEMBER 25

Grant that I may rest in Thee above all things desired, and that my heart may be at peace in Thee.

Thou art the true peace of the heart, Thou art its only rest; outside of Thee all things are hard and uneasy.

Bk. III, ch. xv.

> Oh! would that all this world doth hold
>   Might, as the ebbing tide,
> Depart from me! I need it not,
>   For Thou art at my side.
> If Thou shouldst leave me, Lord, and hide
>   Thy face from me awhile,
> My song of love shall not be stilled,
>   Nor lips forbear to smile.

P.

SEPTEMBER 26

Be fervent therefore in thy spiritual progress, for thou shalt shortly receive the reward of thy labours; and then grief and fear shall no more come near thee.

Thou shalt labour now a little, and thou shalt find great rest, yea, everlasting joy. If thou continue faithful and fervent in working, God will doubtless be faithful and liberal in rewarding. The greater violence thou offerest to thyself, the greater progress thou wilt make.

Bk. I, ch. xxv.

She had unusual courage. From the time she entered Carmel at the age of fifteen she kepe the Rule, apart from fasting, in all its rigour. Her companions in the novitiate, noticing her pallor, would sometimes beg for her to be excused from Matins or the early morning Office, but the Prioress would refuse, saying: "She is not the type who wants dispensations; God is her support, and we must leave her to Him, and not treat her like a child. Besides, if she is ill she should come and say so herself."

But the Saint's maxim was not to give way or complain until she had reached the limit of her strength. Many a time she went to Matins feeling giddy, or with a severe headache. "I am still able to walk," she would say, "so I ought to be at my duties."

Her energy gave her the strength to perform these heroic acts quite simply.

H.

SEPTEMBER 27

Son, thou must diligently make it thy aim that in every place, and in every action or outward employment, thou must be inwardly free and master of thyself; and that all things be under thee, and not thou under them.

That thou mayest be lord and ruler of thy actions, not a slave or bondsman, but rather a freeman and a true Hebrew, transferred to the lot and to the liberty of the children of God. Who stand above the things present and contemplate those that are eternal: who look upon passing things with the left eye, and with the right those of heaven.

Bk. III, ch. xxxviii.

We read that in the old days the Jews rebuilt the walls of Jerusalem holding a sword in one hand as they worked with the other (II Esdras, iv, 17). That is a figure of what we should do: work hard with one hand and with the other ward off dissipation of mind, which would hinder our union with God.

C.

SEPTEMBER 28

Son, I have said, *Peace I leave with you, my peace I give unto you, not as the world giveth, do I give unto you* (John xiv, 27). Peace is what all desire; but all care not for those things which appertain to true peace. My peace is with the humble and meek of heart.

Bk. III, ch. xxv.

During her agony she said: "Mother, prepare me to make a good death." Her Prioress encouraged her with these words: "My child, you are ready to appear before God, because you have always understood the virtue of humility."

She then unconsciously paid a great tribute to herself, saying: "Yes, I feel that is true; my soul has never sought anything but the truth, I have understood humility of heart."

H.

September 29

Blessed, O Lord, be Thy name for ever, who hast been pleased that this trial and tribulation should come upon me. I cannot fly from it, but must of necessity fly to Thee, that Thou mayest help me and turn it to my good. Lord, I am now in tribulation, and my heart is not at ease: but I am much afflicted with my present suffering.

And now, dear Father, what shall I say? I am taken, Lord, in these straits: Oh, save me from this hour! But for this reason I came unto this hour, that Thou mightest be glorified, when I shall be exceedingly humbled and delivered by Thee.

May it please Thee, O Lord, to deliver me: for, poor wretch that I am, what can I do, and whither shall I go without Thee? Give me patience, O Lord, at this time also. Help me, O my God, and I will not fear, how much soever I may be oppressed.

Bk. III, ch. xxix.

More terrible than her physical sufferings was the mental agony of Gethsemane that came upon her. For several days the infirmarian had noticed a look of anguish on her face, and she kept repeating: "Oh! how we should pray for those in their agony! If you only knew!"

One night she begged the Sister watching by her to sprinkle the bed with holy water, saying: "The devil is close to me; I cannot see him, but I feel him. He is tormenting me, holding me in his iron grasp so that I may find no relief, and trying to drive me to despair by increasing my sufferings. I cannot even pray, I can only look at Our Lady and say: Jesus! I am going through something mysterious; I am suffering for another soul, not myself, and the devil is angry."

The infirmarian lit a blessed candle, and the spirit of darkness fled, to return no more. The Saint was undergoing the final assaults of Satan, sometimes directed against those who have opposed his reign.

H.

SEPTEMBER 30

Let me be possessed by love, going above myself through excess of fervour and ecstasy. Let me sing the canticle of love, let me follow Thee, my Beloved, on high; let my soul lose herself in Thy praises, rejoicing exceedingly in Thy love.

Bk. III, ch. v.

Made ready by this martyrdom to come before Thee, may it at length cause my death and suffer my soul to pass into the eternal embrace of Thy merciful love. I wish to renew this offering, O my Beloved, an infinite number of times at every heart-beat, until the shadows flee away and I may tell Thee of my love face to face for all eternity.

Act of Oblation.

I do not regret having offered myself up as a victim to Love.

N.V.

My God . . . I love Thee!

(Her last words).

OCTOBER 1

Enlighten me, O Good Jesus, with the brightness of internal light, and cast out all darkness from the dwelling of my heart.

Bk. III, ch. xxiii.

"From the age of three I have never refused God anything, but I cannot glory in that. You see how the sunset is gilding the tree-tops; because my soul is bathed in the light of divine Love, it appears to shine in your sight, but if the Sun of Justice withheld His rays, I should at once be plunged into darkness."

"What must we do to shine with a golden light?"

"Practise little, lowly virtues. They are not always easy, but God never denies us the first grace to overcome ourselves, and if the soul responds, she at once finds the light. I was always struck by the words of praise addressed to Judith: *Thou hast done manfully, and thy heart has been strengthened* (Judith xv, 11). One must first act courageously, then the soul goes from victory to victory."

C.

OCTOBER 2

O that this day would shine upon us, and all those temporal things come to an end! . . . Blessed is the man who for Thee, O Lord, lets go all things created; who offers violence to his nature, and through fervour of spirit crucifies the lusts of the flesh; that so, his conscience being cleared up, he may offer to Thee pure choirs of angels, having shut out all things of the earth both from without and within.

Bk. III, ch. xlviii.

Dear Angel, given by God to be
   My brother and my friend,
Beneath the shadow of your wings
   May I reach journey's end.
I too shall sing, when breaks the dawn,
   —Eternity's bright day—
With angel choirs the song of praise
   You taught me in the way.

P.

OCTOBER 3

Far more noble is that learning which flows from above, from the divine influence, than that which with labour is acquired by the industry of man.

Bk. III, ch. xxxi.

I asked her what was the spiritual teaching she would impart to souls after her death: "It is the way of spiritual childhood, the way of trust and complete surrender. I will teach them the little practices I have found so successful, make them understand that there is only one thing to do here on earth: scatter the flowers of little sacrifices at Our Lord's feet; win Him by the tenderness of our love. That is how I won His Heart, and why I shall receive such a welcome."

N.V.

O<small>CTOBER</small> 4

The humble man God protects and delivers: the humble He loves and comforts: to the humble He inclines Himself: to the humble He gives grace, and after he has been depressed, raises him to glory.

Bk. II, ch. ii.

Something had occurred which caused her pain, so in order to take her mind off the matter, she asked gently: "Would you read me some Saint's life? I need some food for my soul."

"Would you like the life of St Francis of Assisi? You would enjoy that, he speaks of flowers and birds."

"Not on that account," she replied gravely, "I want his example of humility."

N.V.

O<small>CTOBER</small> 5

God has so disposed things, that we may learn to bear one another's burdens; for there is no man without defect; no man without his burden; no man sufficient for himself; no man wise enough for himself; but we must support one another, comfort one another, assist, instruct, and admonish one another.

Bk. I, ch. xvi.

Imperfect souls are usually left alone; one keeps within the bounds of religious politeness, but one avoids their company from fear of offending them. When I speak of imperfect souls, I do not mean spiritual imperfections—for even the holiest will not be perfect until they reach Heaven—I am referring to lack of judgement or education, to the touchiness of certain characters, all those things which make life so unpleasant for others.

I know that these defects are incurable, but if I were ill for years, my Mother would not for that reason give up nursing me. I have therefore come to this conclusion: I ought to seek the company of those Sisters who please me least, and be a good Samaritan to them. Very often a kind look or a smile is all that is needed to cheer one who is sore and sad at heart. I must not, however, do this simply out of a desire to console others, for I would soon get discouraged, as a word said with the best intentions can so easily be taken up wrongly. I will try to do it solely to please Our Lord and obey His injunction in the Gospel: *When thou makest a dinner, call not thy friends, nor thy kinsmen, nor thy neighbours who are rich; lest perhaps they also invite thee again, and a recompense be made to thee.*

But when thou makest a feast, call the poor, the maimed, the lame, and the blind; and thou shalt be blessed, because they have not wherewith to make thee recompense: for recompense shall be made thee at the resurrection of the just (Luke xiv, 12-14).

H.

OCTOBER 6

Depart from me, thou wicked impostor; thou shalt have no share in me; but my Jesus will be with me, as a valiant warrior, and thou shalt be confounded. I had rather die, and undergo any torment whatsoever, than yield to thy suggestions. Be silent, I will hear no more of thee, although thou so often strive to be troublesome to me. *The Lord is my light and my salvation: whom shall I fear? If armies in camp should stand together against me, my heart shall not fear* (Ps. xxvi, 1-3).

Bk. III, ch. vi.

I bless Thee, O heavenly Father, Father of my Lord
Jesus Christ; because Thou hast vouchsafed to be
mindful of so poor a wretch as I am. O Father of
mercies and God of all comfort, I give thanks to Thee
who sometimes art pleased to cherish with Thy consolation, me, that am unworthy of any comfort. I bless
Thee and glorify Thee for evermore, together with Thy
only-begotten Son, and the Holy Ghost, the Comforter,
to all eternity.

Ibid., ch. v.

Last night I was in great anguish of mind, and my
spiritual darkness increased. I seemed to hear an
accursed voice saying: "How can you be sure that
God loves you? Has He told you so? The opinion of
a few human beings is not going to justify you in His
sight."

I had been a prey to these thoughts for some time
when your truly providential note was handed to me.
In it you recalled the special graces Our Lord has
bestowed on me, and, as though you knew of my
distress, assured me that God loves me dearly and was
about to crown me for all eternity.

Peace and joy began to return to my soul, but I said
to myself: It is my little Mother's love for me that
prompts her to write this.

At that moment I felt inspired to open the Gospels,
and chanced upon these words that I had never noticed
before: *He whom God has sent, speaketh the words of
God: for God doth not give the Spirit by measure* (John
iii, 34). I then fell asleep quite comforted. God has sent
you to me, and I must believe you, as you say the same
things that He does.

H.

OCTOBER 7

Thou hast not here a lasting city; and wherever thou art, thou art a stranger and a pilgrim: nor wilt thou ever have rest, unless thou be interiorly united to Christ.

Bk. II, ch. i.

This life is but a ship that bears thee on, and not thy dwelling-place.
When quite a child these words were always an encouragement to me. Even now, when childish impressions have faded, the thought of a ship helps me to endure my exile on earth. Wisdom herself says: *All those things are passed away like a shadow, and as a ship that passeth through the waves* (Wisd. v, 9, 10).

These thoughts lead me to Infinity, and I seem to see the shores of eternity, to feel the embrace of Christ, Our Lady's welcome, to see my father and mother coming to meet me with four little angels—my brothers and sisters. I enjoy in advance the only true and everlasting home-life.

H.

OCTOBER 8

Leave consolations to God, to do with them as best pleaseth Him. But prepare thou thyself to bear tribulations, and account them the greatest consolations.

Bk. II, ch. xii.

I teach to despise earthly things, to loathe things present, to seek things eternal, to relish things eternal, to fly honours, to endure scandals, to repose all hope in Me, to desire nothing out of Me, and above all things ardently to love Me.

Bk. III, ch. xliii.

You must not think that spiritual consolations are my lot; my one joy is to lack all comfort on earth. Although I never see Him or hear Him, Our Lord is all the time secretly teaching me. He does not do this through books, for I never understand what I read. Sometimes, however, I happen on a word which comforts me, as for instance this evening, after I had spent my time of prayer in much dryness of spirit: *Behold the Master I give you, he will teach you all that you must do. I would have you read the Book of life, in which is found the science of love.*

How sweetly those words sounded to the ears of my soul—the science of love!

H.

OCTOBER 9

Behold, our King marches before us, who will fight for us. Let us follow Him like men of courage; and not shrink through fear. Let us be ready valiantly to die in battle, and not suffer our glory to be tarnished by flying from the standard of the Cross.

Bk. III, ch. lvi.

> He speaketh victory who seeks
>   In all things to obey;
> O God of victories, my will
>   Here at Thy feet I lay!
> I face undaunted shot and shell,
>   My weapon in my hand,
> And singing go to meet my death,
>   For at Thy side I stand.

P.

OCTOBER 10

When he shall have done all things which he knows should be done, let him think that he has done nothing.

Let him not make great account of that which may appear much to be esteemed, but let him in truth acknowledge himself to be an unprofitable servant; as Truth itself has said: *When ye shall have done all these things that are commanded you, say: we are unprofitable servants* (Luke xvii, 10).

Bk. II, ch. xi.

I told her how sad I felt at the thought of appearing before God with empty hands.

She replied: "Although in the same situation, I do not feel like that. Even if I had accomplished the works of St Paul, I should still consider myself an unprofitable servant with empty hands. It is just because I have nothing that I am happy, for I shall receive everything from God."

N.V.

OCTOBER 11

Bow down thyself then humbly at present under the hands of all, and heed not who it was that has said or commanded this. But let it be thy great care, that whether thy superior, or inferior, or equal, desire anything of thee, or hint at anything, thou take all in good part, and labour with a sincere will to perform it.

Bk. III, ch. xlix.

He that has true and perfect charity seeks himself in no one thing, but desires only the glory of God in all things.

Bk. I, ch. xv.

I remember an act of charity God inspired me to do when I was only a novice. Although apparently trifling, our Heavenly Father *who seeth in secret* has already rewarded me in this life. It was before Sœur St. Pierre became a complete invalid. At ten minutes to six someone had to interrupt her prayer to take her to the refectory. It cost me much to offer my services, as I knew how difficult it was to please her, but I did not want to lose this good opportunity, remembering Our Lord's words: *As long as you did it to one of these my least brethren, you did it to me* (Matt. xxv, 40). My offer was accepted, and I set to work with such good will that I succeeded perfectly. Every evening when I saw her take up her hour-glass, I knew that this was the signal to start.

Bracing my courage I began the long ceremony; the bench had to be removed in a certain way, without haste, and then we started off. I had to walk behind, holding her up by her girdle, but if she stumbled she at once thought that I was not holding her properly, and would let her fall: "Oh dear! you are going too quickly, all my bones will be broken!" If I went more slowly, it was: "Why don't you follow me? I can't feel your hand; you will let go and I shall fall! Didn't I say that you were too young to help me!"

At length we would reach the refectory. Once there, fresh difficulties would arise: I had to get her into her place without offending her in any way, turn back her sleeves, and then I might leave her. I soon noticed that she found great difficulty in cutting her bread, so I did this before leaving. This little attention finally won her heart, as she had not asked me to do it; but I learnt later that what pleased her most was the affectionate smile I gave her after finishing my duties.

H.

OCTOBER 12

Ah! if a man had but one spark of perfect charity, he would doubtless perceive that all earthly things are full of vanity.

Bk. I, ch. xv.

Then shall the poor cottage be more commended than the gilded palace.

Bk. I, ch. xxiv.

Although that act of charity was done so long ago, its memory is still fragrant, like a little breeze from Heaven. One winter's evening, cold and dark, when doing this humble duty I suddenly heard the strains of an orchestra in the distance. I saw in imagination a drawing-room, brilliantly lighted, where fashionably dressed young girls were displaying their social graces. Then I looked at my poor invalid; instead of music I only heard plaintive groans; instead of gilded walls, I saw in the dim light the bare bricks of our cloister. The contrast impressed me deeply; the murky light of earthly pleasures was darkness compared to the light of Truth which enlightened my soul, and I would not have given ten minutes spent on my act of charity to purchase a thousand years of worldly pleasures.

H.

OCTOBER 13

Let the least be unto thee as something very great, and the most contemptible as a special favour.

Bk. II, ch. x.

She had a delicate digestion, and found the frugal fare at Carmel a hardship; some dishes actually made her ill, but as she hid the fact, no one knew it. A neighbour of hers at table tried in vain to discover her preferences, and the kitchen Sisters, knowing how easy she was to please, invariably served her with scraps and leavings. It was only during her last illness, when she was obliged to say what food upset her, that her mortification was discovered.

H.

OCTOBER 14

The Lord bestows His blessing there where He finds
the vessels empty: and the more perfectly one forsakes
these things below, and the more he dies to himself by
the contempt of himself, the more speedily grace
cometh, entereth in more plentifully, and the higher it
elevateth the free heart.

Bk. IV, ch. xv.

"Oh! how much I have still to acquire!"
"Say rather *to lose.* God will fill your heart in the
measure that you empty it of imperfections. I can see
that you have missed your way, and will never reach
your goal. You think only of scaling heights, whilst
Our Lord wants you to go down: He is waiting for
you in the fertile valley of humility."

C.

OCTOBER 15

Would to God thou wert worthy to suffer something
for the name of Jesus! How great a glory would be laid
up for thee, how great joy would it be to all the saints
of God, and how great edification to thy neighbour!

Bk. II, ch. xii.

One of the nuns was looking worn out, and I remarked
to the Saint that I could not bear to see suffering,
especially in saintly souls. "I do not feel like that," she
replied, "I never pity saints who suffer. I know that
they have the grace to endure, and that they give glory
to God; but I pity those who are not holy and who
waste their sufferings. They are indeed to be pitied, and
I would do anything to help and encourage them."

C.

OCTOBER 16

There is scarce any one thing in which thou standest so much in need of mortifying thyself, as in seeing and suffering the things which are repugnant to thy will; and especially when that is commanded which seems to thee incongruous and to little purpose. And because being under authority thou darest not resist the higher power, therefore thou art apt to think it hard to walk at the beck of another, and wholly give up thy own sentiment.

Bk. III, ch. xlix.

She told me that once, when second portress, she was told to prepare a night-light for outside in circumstances which should not have arisen, and when she had not the necessary materials at hand. The struggle within her soul was so sharp, that she had to beg most earnestly for grace to overcome herself. She then began the work, giving to it the hour of silence before Matins:

"I imagined that I was preparing a night-light for Our Lady and the Child Jesus, so I worked with the utmost care, removing the least speck of dust, and little by little great peace and consolation filled my soul. When the bell rang for Matins I was not able to go at once, but I had received a special grace, and had Sister N. come and told me that I had made a mistake, and must prepare another light, I would have obeyed gladly.

"From that time I made up my mind not to question whether an order given me were reasonable or not."

N.V.

OCTOBER 17

Lord, in the sincerity of my heart, I offer myself to Thee this day, to be Thy servant evermore, to serve

Thee, and to become a sacrifice of perpetual praise to Thee.

Receive me with this sacred oblation of Thy precious Body, which I offer to Thee this day, in the presence of Thy angels invisibly standing by, that it may be for mine and all the people's salvation.

Bk. IV, ch. ix.

OUR Lord's love for us is so incomprehensible, so delicate, that He will do nothing without us; He wishes us to share with Him in the salvation of souls. The Creator of the universe waits for the prayer, the self-immolation of one poor little soul to save a multitude of others, redeemed, as she was, by the Precious Blood.

E.

OCTOBER 18

They that love Jesus for Jesus' sake, and not for any comfort of their own, bless Him no less in tribulation and anguish of heart, than in the greatest consolation.

Bk. II, ch. xi.

We had prayed fervently to obtain some relief for her, but our petition was not granted. She was able to say: "In spite of my feelings at first, I assured my Heavenly Father and all the Saints that I loved them more than ever."

N.V.

OCTOBER 19

Behold, all things are Thine which I have, and with which I serve Thee. Thou hast beyond all hope shown mercy to Thy servant; and beyond all my desert bestowed Thy grace and friendship on me. Unspeakable, indeed, is the sweetness of Thy contemplation, which Thou bestowest on those that love Thee.

Bk. III, ch. x.

Not for them only do I pray, but for them also who through their word shall believe in me. Father, I will that where I am, they also whom thou hast given me may be with me . . . that the world may know that thou hast loved them, as thou hast also loved me (John xvii, 20, 23).

I wish to repeat these words after Thee before I die. It may be presumption, but Thou hast encouraged me to be daring. As the father of the prodigal said to his elder son: *All I have is thine* (Luke xv, 31), so Thy words belong to me, and I am free to use them to draw down blessings upon the souls that I call mine.

O my God, my one desire, the only glory I seek is to love Thee alone. Thy love went before me in childhood, it has grown with me, and now it is become so great that I cannot fathom its depths.

H.

OCTOBER 20

He that seeks here any other thing than purely God and the salvation of his soul, will find nothing but trouble and sorrow. Neither can he long remain in peace who does not strive to be the least, and subject to all.

Bk. I, ch. xvii.

She once said to a young nun working in the infirmary: "If we are truly humble, we readily obey all without distinction. You should consider yourself not merely the little handmaid of the sick, but a slave whom everyone has the right to command, and whose servile condition makes any thought of complaint out of the question."

E.

OCTOBER 21

When a man of good will is troubled or tempted, or afflicted with evil thoughts, then he better understands what need he hath of God, without whom he finds he can do no good. Then also he laments, he sighs and prays, by reason of the miseries which he suffers.

Bk. I, ch. xii.

It is often the purest souls who are the most assailed by temptations and kept in spiritual darkness. They think that they have lost their spotless purity, and that the thorns that surround them have torn their petals. But it is the lilies among thorns that are the most carefully guarded, and in whom Our Lord takes delight: *Blessed is the man that endureth temptation* (James i, 12).

L.

OCTOBER 22

The sweetness of Thy words invites me, but the multitude of my offences weighs me down. Thou commandest me to approach to Thee with confidence; if I would have part with Thee; and to receive the food of immortality if I desire to obtain life and glory ever-lasting. *Come*, Thou sayest to me, *all ye that labour and are burdened, and I will refresh you* (Matt. xi, 28).

O sweet and amiable word in the ear of a sinner, that Thou, O Lord my God, shouldst invite the poor and needy to the communion of Thy most sacred Body! But who am I, O Lord, that I should presume to come to Thee? Behold, the heaven of heavens cannot contain Thee, and Thou sayest: *Come ye all to Me!*

Bk. IV, ch. i.

My way is not that of fear; I can always manage to be happy, and to profit by my misfortunes, and Our Lord encourages me to persevere in this spirit. I am never troubled by scruples before Holy Communion, but one morning I happened to feel some anxiety. For several days an insufficient number of hosts had been consecrated, and I had received only a fragment. On this particular morning I thought to myself, somewhat unreasonably: If I am given only half a host, I shall think that Our Lord finds no pleasure in coming to me.

What was my delight when the priest gave me two separate hosts! What a consoling answer to my fears!

H.

OCTOBER 23

If thou wilt enter into life, keep the commandments (Matt. xix, 17).

Son, now thou knowest these things, and hast read them all, happy shalt thou be if thou fulfil them. *He that hath my commandments and keepeth them, he it is that loveth me, and I will love him, and I will manifest myself unto him* (John xiv, 21), *and I will make him sit with me in the kingdom of my Father* (Apoc. iii, 21).

Lord Jesus, as Thou hast said and hast promised, so may it be indeed; and may it be my lot to merit it.

Bk. III, ch. lvi.

Sœur Marie du Sacré-Cœur said to her: "What a happy thing it is to die when one has spent one's life in loving!"

"Yes, but to enjoy this happiness one must also have practised fraternal charity."

N.V.

OCTOBER 24

The better thou disposest thyself for suffering, the more wisely dost thou act, and the more dost thou merit; and thou wilt bear it more easily, thy mind being well prepared for it, and accustomed to it.

Bk. III, ch. xix.

> How sweetly doth mine own soul echo,
>   Jesu, those brave words of Thine
> Full of longing for Thy Passion,
>   All on fire with love divine!

P.

OCTOBER 25

When thou shalt arrive thus far, that tribulation becomes sweet and savoury to thee for the love of Christ; then think that it is well with thee, for thou hast found a paradise upon earth.

Bk. II, ch. xii.

Long ago suffering became a paradise on earth for me, and I cannot imagine how I shall become acclimatized in a land where all is happiness without a trace of sorrow. Our Lord will have to transform my soul, otherwise it will not be able to bear eternal bliss.

E.

OCTOBER 26

If thou seek thy comfort and thy gain in others, thou wilt often meet with loss. If in all things thou seek Jesus, doubtless thou wilt find Jesus; but if thou seek thyself, thou wilt indeed find thyself, but to thine own ruin.

Bk. II, ch. vii.

Grace loves even her enemies.

Bk. III, ch. liv.

Our Lord explains His new commandment clearly in the Gospel. We read in St. Matthew: *You have heard that it hath been said: thou shalt love thy neighbour, and hate thy enemy. But I say to you, Love your enemies, do good to them that hate you, and pray for them that persecute and calumniate you* (Matt. v. 43, 44).

We do not find enemies, needless to say, at Carmel, but there are natural attractions; we feel drawn to one Sister, whereas we would go out of our way to avoid meeting another. But Our Lord teaches me that it is this very one that I should love and pray for, even though her manner shows that she dislikes me. *If you love them that love you, what thanks are to you? for sinners also love those that love them* (Luke vi, 32).

It is not enough to love, we must prove our love. We take delight in pleasing a friend, but this is not charity; even sinners do as much.

H.

OCTOBER 27

Give me patience, O Lord, at this time also. Help me, O my God, and I will not fear, how much soever I may be oppressed. And now, in the midst of these things, what shall I say? Lord, Thy will be done; I have well deserved to be afflicted and troubled. I must needs bear it, and would to God it may be with patience, till the storm pass over, and it be better.

But Thy almighty hand is able to take away from me this temptation also, and to moderate its violence, as Thou hast often done heretofore for me, lest I quite sink under it, O my God, my mercy!

Bk. III, ch. xxix.

Our Lord never asks any sacrifice from us that is beyond our strength, though sometimes He allows us to taste all the bitterness of the chalice He holds to our lips. When He asks for all that we hold most dear on earth, it is impossible—short of a special grace—not to cry out as He did in Gethsemane: *Father . . . let this chalice pass from me*, but let us add: *Nevertheless not as I will but as thou wilt* (Matt. xxvi, 3). It is a great consolation to think that Jesus, the God of strength, has known our weakness and trembled at the prospect of His bitter chalice, which before He had so ardently desired.

You are indeed blessed, for Our Lord has called you, and has Himself drunk first of the chalice He now offers you. A saint once said: *The greatest honour God can show a soul is to ask much from her, rather than to give her much.* Our Lord is giving you the privilege of beginning your apostolate already, and of saving souls by your sufferings. Was it not by suffering and death that He redeemed the world? I know that you long to give your life for Him, but martyrdom of the heart is no less fruitful than that of blood, and it is already yours. I have reason to call your lot blessed and worthy of an apostle of Christ.

L.

OCTOBER 28

In some cases you must use violence, and manfully resist the sensual appetite, and not regard what the flesh has a mind for, or what it would fly from; but rather labour that whether it will or not, it may become subject to the spirit.

And so long must it be chastised and kept under servitude, until it readily obey in all things, and learn to be content with a little, and to be pleased with what is plain and ordinary, and not to murmur at any inconvenience.

Bk. III, ch. xi.

One evening after Compline I searched in vain for our lamp on the shelf where they were all kept; as it was during the night-silence I could not ask who had taken it, though I realized that it must have been by mistake. I had counted on working hard that evening, but instead, saw myself condemned to spend a whole hour in the dark. If I had not had the light of grace, I would certainly have complained, but with it I was happy to think that poverty does not only consist in being denied agreeable things, but even those that are necessary. Whilst all was dark around me, my soul was filled with a divine light.

H.

OCTOBER 29

Give Thyself to me, and it is enough: for without Thee no comfort is available. Without Thee I cannot subsist; and without Thy visitation I cannot live.

Bk. IV, ch. iii.

> No charm I find, nor happiness,
> Upon this earth, so bleak and drear.
> Jesus! to Thee I lift mine eyes,
> And to my only Joy draw near.

P.

OCTOBER 30

Ask not for what is delightful and commodious for thee, but what is pleasing and honourable to Me; for if thou judgest rightly thou oughtest to follow My appointment rather than thy own desire, and to prefer it before all that thou desirest.

Bk. III, ch. xlix.

"The thought of soon going to Heaven does not disturb my peace. I am very happy, but I cannot say that I feel any transports of joy."

"But would you not rather die than live?"

"O my little Mother! I repeat what I have said before, that I have no preferences. What pleases me best is what God prefers and chooses for me."

N.V.

OCTOBER 31

God is able to do more than man can understand.

Blessed is that simplicity that leaveth the difficult ways of dispute, and goeth on in the plain and sure path of God's commandments. It is faith that is required of thee, and a sincere life; not the height of understanding, nor diving deep into the mysteries of God.

God never deceiveth; but he is deceived that trusts too much in himself. God walketh with the simple, and revealeth Himself to the humble; He giveth understanding to little ones, openeth the gate of knowledge to pure minds, and hideth His grace from the curious and proud.

Bk. IV, ch. xviii.

I have always longed to be a saint, but when I compared myself with the Saints, I was conscious of the same difference that exists between a high mountain and a grain of sand. Instead of feeling discouraged, I would say to myself: God would never inspire me with an ideal that cannot be attained, so that I can still aspire to sanctity although I am so small and weak. I cannot become great; I must put up with myself as I am, with my innumerable imperfections, but I will try to find a new way to Heaven, quite short and direct. We live in an age of inventions; in the houses of the rich you go up in a lift, instead of climbing the stairs. As I am too small to climb the arduous ladder of perfection, I also must find a lift to carry me up to God.

I turned to the Scriptures to find some clue, and came upon these words from the lips of eternal Wisdom: *Whosoever is a little one, let him come to me* (Prov. ix, 4). Having drawn near to God, I felt sure that I had found what I sought, but to discover what He would do to the *little one*, I read on: *You shall be carried at the breasts, and upon the knees they shall caress you. As one whom the mother caresseth so will I comfort you* (Is. lxvi, 12, 13).

Never had more touching and tender words sounded in my ears. Thy arms, O Jesus, are the *lift* which will carry me up to Heaven! There is no need for me to grow up; I must now remain a *little one* more than ever. Thou hast gone beyond my desire, O my God, and I will praise Thy mercy! *Thou hast taught me, O God, from my youth: and till now I will declare thy wonderful works, unto old age and grey hairs* (Ps. lxx, 17).

H.

November 1

I am He who made all the saints; I gave them grace; I have brought them to glory. I know the first and the last; I embrace them all with an inestimable love.

I am to be praised in all My saints; I am to be blessed above all things, and to be honoured in every one of them, whom I have thus gloriously magnified and eternally chosen, without any foregoing merits of their own.

Take heed, therefore, my son, that thou treat not curiously of these things which exceed thy knowledge, but rather make it thy business and thy aim that thou mayest be found amongst the number of those who inherit the kingdom of God, although thou shouldst be the least amongst them.

Bk. III, ch. lviii.

For a long time I wondered why God has His preferences, and why souls did not all receive the same measure of grace. I was astonished that great sinners like St Paul, St Augustine and St Mary Magdalen should be granted such extraordinary favours, and almost forced to accept them. When reading the Lives of the Saints I could not understand why Our Lord treated some as privileged souls even in their cradles, removing any obstacles that might keep them from Him, and preserving unspotted their baptismal innocence, whilst on the other hand innumerable savages died without ever hearing the name of God.

Jesus Himself taught me this mystery. He laid open before me the book of Nature, and I understood that all the flowers He has created are beautiful; that the loveliness of the rose and the purity of the lily in no way lessen the sweet scent of the hidden violet or the appealing simplicity of the daisy. I understood that if all the little flowers wanted to be roses, Nature would lose her garb of Spring, and the fields would no longer be starred with little blossoms. It is the same in the domain of souls, the living garden of the Lord.

H.

NOVEMBER 2

Lord, I offer to Thee all my sins and offences, which I have committed in Thy sight and that of Thy holy angels, from the day that I was first capable of sin until this hour, upon Thy propitious altar, that Thou mayest burn and consume them all with the fire of Thy charity, and mayest remove all the stains of my sins, and cleanse my conscience from all offences, and restore to me Thy grace, which I have lost by sin, by fully pardoning me all, and mercifully receiving me to the kiss of peace.

Bk. IV, ch. ix.

You, who gave me leave to offer myself up to God, know what a flood of grace has poured into my soul from the time of my oblation. Since June 9, 1895, Love has surrounded me on all sides; at every moment of the day the merciful Love of God renews me, purifies me, and leaves no trace of sin on my soul. I cannot bring myself to fear Purgatory; I know that I am not worthy to enter that place of expiation with the Holy Souls, but I also know that the fire of love is more sanctifying than that of Purgatory, that Our Lord does not want us to suffer needlessly, and that He would never inspire me with desires that He does not intend to fulfil.

H.

NOVEMBER 3

Oh, now exceedingly necessary is Thy grace for me, O Lord, to begin that which is good, to go forward with it, and to accomplish it! Without it I can do nothing: but I can do all things in Thee, strengthened by Thy grace.

Bk. III, ch. lv.

You told me to feed your lambs, as Our Lord once said to St Peter (she was novice-mistress in all but name). I was astonished, thinking myself incapable, and begged you to feed them yourself, allowing me to be of their number. Giving way to some extent, you named me first amongst them, rather than their mistress.

How is it that my youth and inexperience caused you no anxiety? There are few souls on earth who do not measure God's omnipotence by their own limited ideas. The world will have exceptions everywhere, but denies God the right to make them. It has always been the way of men to assess experience by length of years, for the youthful Psalmist sang: *I am very young and despised* (Ps. cxviii, 141). But in the same psalm he says: *I have had understanding above ancients: because I have sought thy commandments. Thy word is a lamp, and a light to my paths. I am ready and am not troubled.*

H.

NOVEMBER 4

Be not solicitous for the shadow of a great name; neither seek to be familiarly acquainted with many, nor to be particularly loved by men. For these things beget distractions and great darkness in the heart.

Bk. III, ch. xxiv.

Nature rejoices in a multitude of friends and kindred; she glories in the nobility of her stock and descent: she fawns on them that are in power, flatters the rich and applauds such as are like herself.

But grace loves even her enemies, and is not puffed up with having a great many friends, nor has any value for family or birth, unless when joined with greater virtue.

Bk. III, ch. liv.

Céline and I found ourselves in the midst of Society people, who made up the bulk of the pilgrimage, but we were not in the least dazzled by their titles. I understood the reference in the Imitation to *the shadow of a great name,* and that greatness is not to be found in a name, but in the soul. Isaias says that: *The Lord God shall call his servants by another name* (Is. lxv, 15), and we read in the Apocalypse: *To him that overcometh I will give a white counter, and in the counter a new name written, which no man knoweth but he that receiveth it*

(Apoc. ii, 17). It is only when we reach Heaven that we shall learn what are our titles of nobility, for *then shall every man have praise from God* (I Cor. iv, 5). He who chose to be poor and unknown on earth for the love of Christ will then be the first, the richest, and the most noble.

H.

NOVEMBER 5

Love is swift, sincere, pious, pleasant, and delightful; strong, patient, faithful, prudent, long-suffering, courageous, and never seeking itself: for where a man seeks himself, there he falls from love.

Bk. III, ch. v.

She knew that whilst we are upon this earth prayer may sometimes be wearisome, but that to persevere in it in spite of fatigue, is to unite ourselves to Our Lord in His agony in the garden. To a novice who told her that she was looking forward to her retreat as it would mean a peaceful rest, she said: "So you are going into retreat in order to enjoy a rest? I am going that I may give myself more completely to God. Remember what is said in the Imitation: *Where a man seeks himself, there he falls from love.*"

E.

NOVEMBER 6

Above all things, and in all things, do thou, my soul, rest always in the Lord, for He is the eternal rest of the saints. Because, indeed, my heart cannot truly rest, nor be entirely contented, till it rest in Thee, and rise above all Thy gifts, and all things created.

Bk. III, ch. xxi.

My will, may all, I do resign
  Into Thy hands, which feed
My soul with hidden manna sweet,
  Fulfilling all my need.
One look from Thee is my reward,
  Thou knowest what is best;
And, safe within Thy arms, my soul
  Shall sleep and take her rest.

P.

November 7

Set thyself, then, like a good and faithful servant of
Christ, to bear manfully the cross of thy Lord, crucified
for the love of thee.

Bk. II, ch. xii.

When I was a postulant I found it very hard to perform certain exterior mortifications customary in our
monasteries, but I never gave way to my repugnance.
The crucifix in the garth seemed to be looking at me
with imploring eyes, begging me to make these sacrifices.

H.

November 8

Many things must thou pass by with a deaf ear, and
think rather of those things that appertain to thy
peace.

It is more profitable to turn away thy eyes from such
things as displease thee, and to leave to everyone his
own way of thinking, than to give way to contentious
discourses. If thou standest well with God, and lookest
to His judgement, thou wilt more easily bear to see
thyself overcome.

Bk. III, ch. xliv.

A certain member of the Community had a way of annoying me by everything she did; the devil must have had a finger in this, by making me see only her unpleasant side, but I would not give way to my antipathy. I said to myself that charity is not merely a matter of feelings, but must be proved by deeds, so I set myself to do for her what I would do for the person most dear to me. Every time I met her I prayed for her, offering up her virtue and merits to God. I knew this pleased Our Lord, for what artist is there who does not like to have his work praised? The divine Artist of souls is pleased when we do not stop at the exterior, but penetrate to the hidden sanctuary which He has chosen for a dwelling-place, and we admire its beauty.

I not only prayed much for the one who caused me many a struggle, but I also tried to be of service to her. When tempted to give her a disagreeable answer, I gave her instead a sweet smile, and tried to turn the conversation, for it is written in the Imitation: *It is more profitable to leave everyone his own way of thinking, than to give way to contentious discourses.*

H.

NOVEMBER 9

It is no great thing to be able to converse with them that are good and meek, for this is naturally pleasing to all, and everyone would willingly have peace, and love those best that agree with them.

But to live peaceably with those that are harsh and perverse, or disorderly, or such as oppose us, is a great grace and a highly commendable and manly exploit.

Bk. II. ch. iii.

Sometimes, when I was more violently tempted than usual, and saw that I would not be able to conceal the struggle, I ran away like a deserter. In spite of this, the Sister for whom I felt a natural aversion said to me one day: "Will you tell me what you like so much in me? Every time I meet you, you give me a gracious smile."

What was it that attracted me? It was Jesus hidden in her soul who could change bitter into sweet.

H.

NOVEMBER 10

A priest should be adorned with all virtues and give example of a good life to others. His conversation should not be with the vulgar and common ways of men, but with the angels in heaven, or with perfect men upon earth.

Bk. IV, ch. v.

Another experience (gained during the pilgrimage) was concerning priests. Up till then I could not understand the chief aim of the Carmelite Reform; the idea of praying for sinners delighted me, but to pray for priests, whose souls, I thought, must be pure as crystal, seemed to me surprising. It was in Italy that I understood my vocation, and it was worth while going so far to learn it.

During the space of a month I came across many holy priests, but although their sublime dignity raises them above the angels, they are nevertheless men with human weaknesses. If then the best of them, the salt of the earth as they are called in the Gospel, are in need of prayers, what of those who are lukewarm? Did not Our Lord say: *If the salt lose its savour, wherewith shall it be salted?* (Matt. v. 13).

H.

NOVEMBER 11

It is a thing not of the least importance to forsake thyself even in the least thing.

Bk. III, ch. xxxix.

Sœur Geneviève had been looking at a box used for sweets at a christening, and remarked that the child's head on the lid would serve her as a model for an angel's head. St Teresa wanted very much to see it, but as no one thought of showing it to her, she made the sacrifice of not asking. I learnt this from her own lips later.

N.V.

NOVEMBER 12

We are men, and but frail men, though by many we are reputed and called angels. Who is the man that is able to keep himself so warily and with such circumspection in all things, as not to fall sometimes into some deceit or perplexity?

But he that trusts in Thee, and seeks Thee with a simple heart, does not so easily fall.

Bk. III, ch. xlv.

> I live by love, and so I guard
>   A precious treasure rare
> Within an earthen vessel frail,
>   And cherish it with care.
> No angel, I, but Eve's poor child,
>   Who hourly fail and fall;
> O everlasting arms uphold!
>   Love, answer Thou my call!

P.

NOVEMBER 13

Make now to thyself friends, by honouring the saints of God, and imitating their actions; that when thou

shalt fail in this life, they may receive thee into everlasting dwellings.

Bk. I, ch. xxiii.

I stood before the Angels and Saints and addressed
them in these words: I am the least of all creatures,
I know my great need, but I also know that noble and
generous hearts love to do good: therefore I beseech of
you, O blessed citizens of Heaven, to adopt me as your
child. Whatever glory I may acquire will redound to
yours. Hear my prayer and obtain for me a double
measure of your love.

H.

November 14

It is no small matter to live in a monastery, or in a
congregation, and to converse therein without reproof,
and to persevere faithfully till death. Blessed is he who
has there lived well, and made a happy end.

Bk. I, ch. xvii.

I do not say: If it be hard to live at Carmel, it is
sweet to die there, but—If it be sweet to live at Carmel,
it is sweeter far to die there.

N.V.

November 15

By degrees, and by patience, with longanimity, thou
shalt by God's grace better overcome than by harshness
and thine own importunity. Deal not roughly with one
that is tempted, but comfort him, as thou wouldst wish
to be done to thyself.

Bk. I, ch. xiii.

During her illness she noticed with what care the
infirmarian chose out the smoothest linen for her use,

and drew this conclusion: We ought to treat suffering souls with the same delicate care, even the most imperfect. How often out of thoughtlessness we wound them by neglect, lack of consideration, discourtesy, when we should be doing our utmost to soothe and comfort them.

N.V.

NOVEMBER 16

No man securely rejoiceth, unless he have within him the testimony of a good conscience. Yet the security of the saints was always full of the fear of God. Neither were they less careful or humble in themselves, because they were shining with great virtues and graces.

Bk. I, ch. xx.

They tell me that I shall be afraid of death; that may well be. If you only knew how diffident I am about myself: I never rely on my own ideas; I know my weakness only too well, but I will take comfort in what Our Lord allows me to feel at the moment. It will be time enough to suffer when I feel differently.

N.V.

NOVEMBER 17

O that with Thy presence thou wouldst enflame, burn, and transform me into Thyself, that I may be made one spirit with Thee, by the grace of internal union and by the melting of ardent love!

Bk. IV, ch. xvi.

If Thy justice loves to stay its course upon earth, how much more must not Thy merciful love wish to enflame souls, for *Thy mercy is in heaven* (Ps. xxxv, 5). O Jesus, may I be the favoured victim . . . consume Thy little host in the fire of divine love!

H.

NOVEMBER 18

Thou must pass through fire and water, before thou comest to refreshment.

Bk. I, ch. xxii.

Before I could *sit down under his shadow, whom I desired* (Cant. ii, 3), I had to go through many trials, but God's call became so insistent, that to answer it I would have passed through fire. The only soul I found to encourage me in my vocation was my beloved Pauline. Her heart was a faithful echo of mine, and without her support I should never have reached the blessed haven which had already sheltered her for five years.

H.

NOVEMBER 19

Nature seeks to have things that are curious and fine, and does not care for things that are cheap and coarse: but grace is pleased with that which is plain and humble, rejects not coarse things, nor refuses to be clad in old clothes.

Bk. III, ch. liv.

Then shall the mean habit shine, and fine clothing appear contemptible.

Bk. I, ch. xxiv.

She had been given a new habit (the one preserved as a relic), and had worn it for the first time at Christmas 1896. It was the second she had had since her Clothing, and it fitted her very badly. I asked if this caused her any annoyance : "Not in the least! No more than if it belonged to a Chinaman thousands of miles away."

N.V.

NOVEMBER 20

Thou knowest, O Lord, what is best; do with me as Thou knowest, and as best pleaseth Thee, and is most for Thy honour.

Put me where Thou wilt, and do with me in all things according to Thy will. I am in Thy hand, turn me round which way Thou wilt.

Bk. III, ch. xv.

For some time past I had offered myself to the Child Jesus to be His little plaything. I asked Him not to treat me like an expensive toy, that children look at but scarcely dare to touch, but like a cheap ball that He could throw on the ground, kick, pierce, leave in the corner, or press to His Heart if He pleased. I wanted to amuse the Child Jesus and give myself up to His childish fancies.

In Rome He heard my prayer, for He pierced His ball . . . no doubt to see what was in it . . . and then, pleased with His discovery, let the ball drop and fell asleep. What was He doing in His sleep, and what became of the forgotten toy?

Jesus dreamt that He was still playing; that He took up the ball, and then let it drop; that He threw it far away, and at last pressed it to His Heart, never to let it out of His little hand again.

H.

NOVEMBER 21

Man beholds the face; but God looks upon the heart.

Man considers the actions; but God weighs the intentions.   Bk. II, ch. vi.

I showed her a photograph of herself: "That is only the envelope; when shall we see the letter? How I would love to see the letter!"

                                                        N.V.

NOVEMBER 22

No chastity is secure without Thy protection. No guard that we can keep upon ourselves will profit us, if Thy holy providence watch not over us.

                                              Bk. III, ch. xiv.

The thought of dear little St Cecilia fills me with delight; what a model she was! In the midst of a pagan world, and at a time of great danger, when she was about to become the bride of a man who had no thoughts of anything higher than earthly love, it seems to me that she should have wept and trembled. Instead of which, *while the musical instruments were playing, Cecilia sang unto the Lord in her heart* (Office of St Cecilia). What sublime trust! No doubt she heard other melodies than those of earth, the divine Bridegroom sang to her, and the angels repeated the refrain they sang on that blessed night: *Glory be to God in the highest, and peace on earth to men of good will!*

The glory of God, how well Cecilia understood it! She sought it with all the ardour of her soul, and knowing how Christ thirsted for souls, longed to bring Him this young Roman. He thought only of earthly glory, but the wise virgin, in whose footsteps so many were to tread, made of him a martyr. She fears nothing: the angels promised and sang of peace; she knew that

the Prince of Peace was bound to protect her, preserve
her virginity, and reward her at the end. *O how beautiful
is the chaste generation with glory* (Wisd. iv, 1).

H.

NOVEMBER 23

Oh! how much is the pure love of Jesus able to do,
when it is not mixed with any self-interest or self-love!
Are not all those to be called hirelings, who are always
seeking consolation? Are they not proved to be rather
lovers of themselves than of Christ, who are always
thinking of their own profit and gain?

Where shall we find a man that is willing to serve
God gratis?

Bk. II, ch. xi.

> I do not serve Thee, Lord, for gain,
>   That were a hireling's way!
> Love does not wait with outstretched hand
>   For payment day by day.
> My heart's love is my only wealth,
>   And this I bring to Thee;
> I only ask that to the end
>   Thy handmaid I may be.

P.

NOVEMBER 24

I will hear what the Lord God will speak to me (Ps.
lxxxiv).

Happy is that soul which heareth the Lord speaking
within her, and from His mouth receiveth the word
of comfort! Happy ears, which receive the accents of
the divine whisper, and take no notice of the whisper-
ings of the world. Happy ears, indeed, which hearken to
Truth itself teaching within, and not to the voice which
soundeth without.

Bk. III, ch. i.

When I was seventeen and eighteen I found much light in the writings of St John of the Cross, and he was my principal guide, but later on all spiritual writers left me in great dryness of spirit, and do so still. However beautiful and moving a book may be, as soon as I begin to read I am incapable of taking it in, and my heart is troubled; or if I do understand, my mind is unable to meditate further. In this state of helplessness the Scriptures and the Imitation come to my assistance, and in them I find a hidden manna, pure and sustaining.

The Gospel is my chief support in prayer, and I find in it all that my poor little soul needs. I am always finding new light there, and hidden, mysterious meanings; I learn by experience that *the kingdom of God is within us* (Luke xvii, 21). The divine Master has no needs of books or other teachers to do His work; He instructs the soul silently, without words. I have never heard Him, but I know that He is within me, inspiring and prompting me at the moment I need it most. It is not usually at my prayer that I see this new light, but when doing my ordinary work during the day.

H.

NOVEMBER 25

A fervent religious man bears and takes all things well that are commanded him. A negligent and lukewarm religious man has trouble upon trouble, and on every side suffers anguish; because he has no comfort within, and is hindered from seeking any without.

A religious man that lives not in discipline lies open to dreadful ruin.

Bk. I, ch. xxv.

How much anxiety our vow of obedience spares us! Simple religious are fortunate beings; as the will of

superiors is their only compass, they can never lose their
way, even if superiors make mistakes. But if a soul
neglects to consult her compass, she will soon wander
off into the desert where no water of grace is to be
found.

H.

NOVEMBER 26

Thou shalt not labour here long, nor shalt thou be
always oppressed with sorrows. Wait a little while, and
thou shalt see a speedy end of all thy evils.

The hour will come when labour and trouble shall be
no more. All is little and short which passeth away
with time.

Bk. III, ch. xlvii.

I need to forget this world, Céline, where everything
wearies me. I can find happiness only in suffering, a
happiness which, though not felt, is above all earthly
joys. This life is passing and eternity draws near, when
we shall live by God's own life, and drink from the
source of all bliss, after having tasted the cup of bitterness here below.

The fashion of this world passeth away (I Cor. vii, 31),
and we shall see new skies, the boundless seas and wide
horizons bathed in the brightness of another sun. With
our Heavenly Bridegroom we shall pass over the waters
playing on our harps, that hung mute *upon the willows*
(Ps. cxxxvi) in the Babylon of our exile, where we were
once captives. Then we shall make melody with joyful
hearts, whereas here *we sat and wept when we remembered
Sion. How shall we sing the song of the Lord in a strange
land* (ibid.)?

L.

NOVEMBER 27

He that loves God with his whole heart neither fears death, nor punishment, nor judgement, nor hell; because perfect love gives secure access to God.

Bk. I, ch. xxiv.

"What would you do if you had to begin your religious life over again?"

"I think I should do just as I have done."

"Then you do not share the feelings of the hermit who said: "No matter how many years I have spent in penance, as long as I have quarter of an hour of life left, and breath in my body, I should be afraid of damnation"?

"No, I do not feel like that, I am too little to be damned; little children do not go to hell."

"You always try to remain as a little child, but tell us how to obtain the spirit of childhood; what does it mean to remain little?"

"It means acknowledging our own nothingness, and looking to God for everything, just as a little child relies entirely on its father. It means not worrying about anything, nor amassing a fortune.'

C.

NOVEMBER 28

If thou wilt be exalted in heaven, humble thyself in this world: If thou wilt reign with Me, bear the cross with Me, for none but the servants of the Cross find the way of bliss and of true light.

Bk. III, ch. lvi.

How meek and humble of heart Thou dost appear, my beloved Saviour, when I look upon Thee hidden under the white Host! Thou couldst not stoop lower in order to teach me humility; I, therefore, in return for Thy love will put myself in the last place and share Thy humiliations, that I may *have a part with Thee* (John xiii, 8) in the kingdom of Heaven.

I beg of Thee to send me a humiliation every time I try to exalt myself above others.

Pr.

NOVEMBER 29

Lord, this is the work of a perfect man, never to let one's mind slacken from attending to heavenly things.

Bk. III, ch. xxvi.

"How do you manage always to be thinking about God?" Sœur Marie du Sacré-Cœur asked her.

"It is natural to think of those one loves; I find no difficulty in doing so."

"Are you then always consciously aware of His presence?"

"Yes; I believe that I have never spent more than three minutes without thinking of Him."

Sum.

NOVEMBER 30

To bear the cross, to love the cross, to chastise the body and bring it under subjection, to fly honours, to be willing to suffer reproaches, to despise one's self, and wish to be despised; to bear all adversities and losses, and to desire no prosperity in this world, is not according to man's natural inclination.

If thou lookest to thyself, thou canst do nothing of this of thyself. But if thou confidest in the Lord,

strength will be given thee from heaven, and the world
and the flesh shall be made subject to thee.

Bk. II, ch. xii.

It is true that it costs us much to give Our Lord what
He is asking, but what joy it is to feel the cost and carry
our cross so weakly! Instead of reproaching Him for
having sent us this cross, I cannot fathom the depths of
divine love which move Him so to treat us. God must
love Father very dearly to send him such suffering.
What joy for us to share this humiliation with him!

I know that the only way to sanctity is by humiliations, and our great trial should prove a veritable gold-
mine for us. I, who am but a little grain of sand, face
the task without courage or strength, but my weakness
will be victorious, as I undertake to do this out of love.
This is the beginning of martyrdom, let us enter the
arena together and offer up our sufferings for the salvation of souls.

L.

DECEMBER 1

The saints and friends of Christ served the Lord in
hunger and thirst; in cold and nakedness; in labour
and weariness; in watchings and fastings; in prayers
and holy meditations; in persecutions and many
reproaches. Alas! what is our life if compared to theirs!

Bk. I, ch. xviii.

Her greatest hardship at Carmel was doing without a
fire in winter. It is easy to imagine what this delicate
child must have endured during the long Norman
winters, in the damp climate of Lisieux. When the
cold was more intense, after having spent the whole day

shivering, the Saint would go and warm herself for a few minutes in the Community room after Matins. But to reach her cell afterwards, she had to walk about forty yards along an open cloister, and the rest of the way up the stairs and down the icy corridor robbed her of the little warmth she had acquired. When she finally lay down on her straw mattress, covered by two thin blankets, she could only get snatches of sleep. Sometimes she spent the whole night awake, shivering with the cold.

If at the beginning of her religious life she had spoken of this to the novice-mistress, she would have been given some relief, but she preferred to endure this severe hardship without complaint. It was only her death-bed that the truth became known, when she admitted: "The greatest physical suffering of my religious life has been from the cold; I suffered from it to such an extent that I nearly died of it."

H.

December 2

Then wilt thou rejoice more that thou hast kept silence, than that thou hast made long discourses, or talked much.

Bk. I, ch. xxiv.

Some time after she came to Carmel she was appointed aid to Sœur Agnès de Jésus, her beloved "Pauline", in the refectory. Knowing that unnecessary speaking was forbidden, she never once allowed herself to say anything intimate.

"Oh! little Mother, how much I went through at that time!" she said later. "I could not tell you what was in my heart, and I thought you no longer knew me."

After five years of this heroic silence, Sœur Agnès was elected Prioress. On the evening of the election "little Thérèse's" heart must have beat with joy at the thought of at length being able to speak freely to her "little Mother", and pour out her soul to her as of old. However, God so permitted that she saw less than any of the nuns of the Prioress.

H.

DECEMBER 3

Aim only at this, pray for this, desire this, that thou mayest be divested of all self-seeking, and thus naked, follow the naked Jesus; that thou mayest die to thyself, and live eternally to Me. Then all vain imagination shall vanish, all evil disturbances and superfluous cares. Then also immoderate fear shall leave thee, and inordinate love shall die.

Bk. III, ch. xxxvii.

A novice had asked several Sisters to help her to shake blankets, adding rather sharply that they must be careful not to tear them, as the blankets were thin and worn. The Saint said to her: "If it did not happen to be your duty to mend the blankets, you would have spoken more gently and shown greater detachment. You ought not to let self-interest colour your actions."

C.

DECEMBER 4

(Christ.) What do I require more of thee than that thou endeavour to resign thyself entirely to Me. Whatsoever thou givest beside thyself I regard not; for I seek not thy gift, but thyself. As it would not suffice thee, if thou hadst all things but Me; so neither can it please

Me, whatever thou givest, as long as thou offerest not thyself. Offer thyself to Me, and give thy whole self for God, and thy offering will be accepted.

Behold, I offered my whole self to the Father for thee, and have given My whole Body and Blood for thy food, that I might be all thine, and thou mightest be always Mine. But if thou wilt not offer thyself freely to My will, thy offering is not perfect, nor will there be an entire union betwixt us.

Bk. IV, ch. viii.

(Disciple.) Lord, all things are Thine that are in heaven and earth. I desire to offer up myself to Thee as a voluntary oblation, and to remain for ever Thine. . . . Behold, I commit myself to Thy mercy; I resign myself into Thy hands. Deal with me according to Thy goodness.

Bk. IV, ch. ix.

Saint Teresa went through great suffering during her life, and for the sake of souls wished this to be made known after her death, so that seeing the seal of the cross upon her life, they might recognize her mission as genuine. She did not, however, consider the martyrdom of the heart which she underwent was a sign of her acceptance as victim by God's merciful Love; it was *the infinite tenderness of divine Love which overflowed from the Sacred Heart into her soul* that she took as a pledge.

If she said that *to offer oneself as a victim of Love is to give oneself up to much anguish and suffering*, it was to souls who held back and would not allow Our Lord to work His whole will in them, as it was often painful; but to souls who, in spite of their shrinking from the cross, were on fire with love and zeal and sought after perfection, she said: *Why are you afraid to offer yourself as a victim to God's merciful Love? I could understand if it were to His Justice, but His merciful Love will have pity on your weakness and will treat you very gently and mercifully.*

H.

DECEMBER 5

To be without Jesus is a grievous hell, and to be with Jesus a sweet paradise.

Bk. II, ch. viii.

I do not know what more I could have in Heaven than I already have on earth, except that I shall see God. As for being with Him, I am that always, even here on earth.

H.

DECEMBER 6

If Thou wilt have me to be in darkness, be Thou blessed; and if Thou wilt have me to be in light, be Thou again blessed; if Thou vouchsafe to comfort me, be Thou blessed; and if it be Thy will I should be afflicted, be Thou always equally blessed.

Bk. III, ch. xvii.

I thank Our Lord for making me walk in darkness, for I do so in much peace. I would willingly spend the whole of my religious life in this dark underground passage, if by it I might win light for sinners.

I am only too glad to be without consolation; I would be ashamed if my love were no better than that of a fiancée in the world, who only looks for presents or admiration. I love my Betrothed for His own sake, and it is His tears and not looks of admiration that I want from Him. I long to wipe away those tears, to gather them up as precious diamonds to adorn my wedding dress.

My heart's desire is to love Jesus as He has never been loved before.

L.

DECEMBER 7

By so much the more does a man draw nigh to God, by how much the farther he withdraw himself from all earthly comfort. So much the higher also he ascends into God, by how much the lower he descends into himself, and by how much the meaner he esteems himself.

But he that attributes anything of good to himself, stops the grace of God from coming into him; for the grace of the Holy Ghost ever seeks an humble heart.

If thou couldst perfectly annihilate thyself, and cast out from thee all created love, abundance of grace would flow into thee.

Bk. III, ch. xlii.

When Our Lord made us go up into the tree, like Zaccheus, He unfolded many mysteries before our eyes. Now let us listen to His words: *Make haste and come down; for this day I must abide in thy house* (Luke xix, 5). Where must we go when we come down? The disciples asked: *Rabbi, where dwellest thou* (John i, 38)? We learn from His own lips that *the foxes have holes, and the birds of the air nests; but the Son of man hath not where to lay his head* (Luke ix, 58). We must therefore go down so low, that in our poverty *we have not where to lay our head,* for then Our Lord will be able to dwell within us

I was given the light to see this during my retreat. Christ wishes us to receive Him into our hearts; they are empty as far as concerns creatures, but mine, alas, is not empty of self, and that is why I am bidden to *go down*. I will go down so low that Jesus will be able to lay His sacred Head upon my heart, and feel that He is understood and loved.

L.

DECEMBER 8

O Lord, teach me to do Thy will, teach me to converse worthily and humbly in Thy sight; for Thou art my wisdom, who knowest me in Truth, and didst know me before the world was made, and before I was born in the world.

Bk. III, ch. iii.

Let Thy will be mine, and let my will always follow Thine, and agree perfectly with it. Let me always will or not will the same with Thee: and let me not be able to will or not will any otherwise than as Thou willest or willest not.

Bk. III, ch. xv.

Our Lady's unique privilege was her Immaculate Conception and divine Motherhood, and yet Our Lord tells us that *whosoever shall do the will of my Father that is in heaven, he is my brother, and sister, and mother* (Matt. xii, 15). It is well to speak of Mary's prerogatives but that is not enough, we must make her loved. If a sermon on her only calls forth "ohs!" and "ahs!" of admiration, it ends by being wearisome, and does not draw us to love and imitate her.

N.V.

DECEMBER 9

Let Thy grace, O Almighty God, assist us, that we who have undertaken the office of priesthood, may serve Thee worthily and devoutly in all purity and good conscience.

Bk. IV, ch. xi.

> Pure as the angel at his side,
>   A soul newborn My priest must be;
> A sister, hidden and unknown,
>   Obtains for him this grace from Me.

P.

DECEMBER 10

At these times it is expedient for thee to fly to humble and exterior works, and to recreate thyself in good actions; to look for My coming and My heavenly visitation with an assured hope; to bear with patience thy banishment, and the aridity of thy mind, till thou be visited again by Me, and delivered from all anguish. I will make thee forget thy pains, and enjoy internal rest.

Bk. III, ch. li.

When we are all at ease within our own souls, we must go out from ourselves. God does not oblige us to remain in our own company when it is distasteful; on the contrary, He sometimes lets us feel how unpleasant we are, in order that we may leave ourselves. I know no other way of going out than by paying a visit to Jesus and Mary by doing acts of charity.

C.

DECEMBER 11

I became the most humble and most abject of all men,

that thou mightest learn to overcome thy pride by my
humility.

Bk. III, ch. xiii.

Lord Jesus, forasmuch as Thy way is narrow and despised by the world, grant that I may follow Thee, and
be despised by the world: for the disciple is not above
the master, nor the servant above his lord (Matt. x, 24).
Let Thy servant meditate on Thy life, for there is my
salvation and true holiness.

Bk. III, ch. lvi.

O Jesus, when a pilgrim upon earth Thou didst say:
*Learn of me because I am meek and humble of heart: and
you shall find rest to your souls* (Matt. xi, 29). My soul
finds rest when I see Thee, the mighty King of Heaven,
humble Thyself in the form of a slave and wash the
feet of Thy disciples. When giving this lesson in
humility Thou didst say: *I have given you an example,
that as I have done to you, so you do also. The servant is
not greater than his lord; neither is the apostle greater
than he that sent him. If you know these things, you shall
be blessed if you do them* (John xii, 15, 16, 17).

I understand these words spoken from the depths of
Thy meek and humble Heart, and with the help of
Thy grace I am resolved to put them into practice.

Pr.

DECEMBER 12

Nature easily complains of want and of trouble: but
grace bears poverty with constancy. This grace is a
supernatural light, and a certain special gift of God, and
the proper mark of the elect, and the pledge of eternal
salvation, which elevates a man from the things of earth

to the love of heavenly things; and of carnal, makes him spiritual.

Wherefore, by how much the more nature is kept down and subdued, with so much the greater abundance grace is infused; and the inward man, by new visitations, is daily more reformed according to the image of God.

Bk. III, ch. liv.

If you lend to them of whom you hope to receive, what thanks are to you? for sinners also lend to sinners, for to receive as much. Do good, and lend, hoping for nothing thereby: and your reward shall be great (Luke vi, 34, 35). Even on earth the reward is very great. It is only the first step that costs, for it seems a hard saying: *lend, hoping for nothing thereby;* it would be easier to give outright.

This is what may sometimes be said to you: "I need your help for a few hours, I have permission to ask you, and will repay the time you give me." You know very well that this will never be done, and would prefer to give your services, making it quite plain that you do not count on the proffered help. It is more generous to give than to lend, and more pleasing to our pride, but how different are the promptings of Nature from the divine teaching! It would be impossible to understand it, let alone practise it, without the help of grace.

H.

DECEMBER 13

Nothing is more acceptable to God, nothing more wholesome for thee in this world, than to suffer willingly for Christ.

Bk. II, ch. xii.

To a novice who was pitying herself she said: "God loves cheerful people who can always manage to smile. When will you learn to hide your troubles, and tell Our Lord with a song on your lips that you are glad to suffer for His sake?"

C.

DECEMBER 14

See thou have God before thine eyes, and do not contend with complaining words. And if at present thou seem to be overcome, and to suffer a confusion which thou hast not deserved, do not repine at this, and do not lessen thy crown by impatience. Rather look up to Me in heaven, who am able to deliver thee from all confusion and wrong, and to repay everyone according to his works.

Bk. III, ch. xxxvi.

You (the Prioress) were ill at the time with bronchitis, and we had been rather anxious about you. One morning I came to the infirmary to return the keys of the Communion grille, as I was sacristan. I was secretly pleased at having an opportunity of seeing you, but another Sister, fearing lest I should wake you, came forward to take the keys herself. I assured her, as politely as I could, that I was just as anxious as she was not to disturb you, but that it was my *right* to return the keys. Today I understand how much more perfect it would have been to have yielded, but not realizing it then, I insisted on going in.

The very thing we wanted to avoid then happened, for the noise made you open your eyes. The Sister made a long speech, the gist of it being that it was my fault that you had been disturbed. I was longing to defend myself, but suddenly had a bright idea. I saw that if I began to excuse myself I would only lose my peace of mind, but that I had too little virtue to refrain from doing so. The only thing left was to run away, which I promptly did. My heart was beating so fast that I was obliged to sit on the stairs and enjoy the fruits of victory for a few minutes. Although this was an odd way of showing my bravery, I thought it better not to engage in combat when defeat was certain.

H.

DECEMBER 15

All self-seekers and self-lovers are bound in fetters, full of desires, full of cares, unsettled, and seeking always their own ease, and not the things of Jesus Christ: but oftentimes devising and framing that which shall not stand. For all shall come to nothing that proceeds not from God.

Take this short and perfect word: *Forsake all, and thou shalt find all, leave thy desires, and thou shalt find rest.* Consider this well, and when thou shalt put it in practice, thou shalt understand all things.

(Disciple.) Lord, this is not the work of one day, nor children's sport; yea, in this one short sentence is included the whole perfection of a religious man.

Bk. III, ch. xxxii.

"How did you come to enjoy such serene and unbroken peace?"

"By forgetting myself, and never seeking myself in anything."

N.V.

DECEMBER 16

What marvel if I should be wholly set on fire by Thee, and should die to myself, since Thou art a Fire always

burning and never decaying, a Love purifying the heart
and enlightening the understanding.

Bk. IV, ch. xvi.

Sœur Marie de l'Eucharistie (her cousin Marie Guérin) had to light the candles for a procession, but having
no matches went to a little lamp before the relics. She
found the wick nearly burnt out, but from the tiny
flame was able to light her own candle and those of the
Community. I thought to myself: Who could take
pride in her own achievements! All these bright flames
came from a dying flicker, and could in their turn give
light to countless others, until the whole world were
ablaze. And yet the origin of the fire would still remain
this modest little lamp. That is like the Communion
of Saints; a little spark is able to produce a great light
in the Church, such as doctors or martyrs. Very often
unknown to us, the light and the graces we receive are
due to some hidden soul, for God wills that the Saints
should obtain graces for each other through prayer, so
that in Heaven they may love one another with a great
love far surpassing that which unites the most ideal
family on earth.

I often think that perhaps I owe all my graces to the
intercession of a humble soul whom I shall only meet
in Heaven.

N.V.

DECEMBER 17

A true lover of Christ and a diligent pursuer of virtue
does not hunt after comforts, nor seek sensible sweetnesses, but is rather willing to bear strong trials and
hard labours for Christ.

Bk. II, ch. ix.

God would have thee learn to suffer tribulation without comfort.

Ibid., ch. xii

I find happiness only in suffering without consolation. It would, however, be seeking your own satisfaction if you wanted to *feel* this happiness or a real taste for suffering, for when we like anything we no longer suffer. We must be prepared to suffer without feeling the courage to do so. If Jesus was sorrowful when He suffered, there can be no suffering without sorrow. We deceive ourselves if we hope to suffer nobly and gracefully.

L.

DECEMBER 18

I offer to Thee all the good I have, though very little and imperfect; that Thou mayest make it better, and sanctify it; that Thou mayest be pleased with it, and make it acceptable to Thee, and perfect it more and more; and mayest moreover bring me, who am a slothful and unprofitable wretch, to a good and happy end.

Bk. IV, ch. ix.

(Christ.) Do what lieth in thee, and do it diligently; not out of custom, nor for necessity, but with fear and reverence and affection. I will supply what is wanting in thee.

Ibid., ch. xii.

Having read the following passage: *All mercy shall make a place for every man according to the merit of his works* (Ecclus. xvi, 15), one of the novices asked her young mistress why there was mention of merit, when St Paul tells us that we are *justified freely by grace* (Rom. iii, 24)?

The Saint explained that although hope pushed to its furthest limits is made up of self-surrender and trust in God, yet it feeds on the spirit of sacrifice: "We must do all in our power, be generous in our efforts, always deny ourselves, in short, prove our love by doing our utmost. But as our achievements are worth very little, it is necessary to put our whole trust in Him who can sanctify our work, and own that we are *unprofitable servants* (Luke xvii, 10), hoping by God's grace to receive what is lacking in us."

E.

DECEMBER 19

It is expedient for thee to look for My coming and My heavenly visitation with an assured hope; to bear with patience thy banishment and the aridity of thy mind, till thou be visited again by Me and delivered from all anguish.

I will make thee forget thy pains and enjoy internal rest. I will lay open before thee the pleasant fields of the Scriptures, that thy heart being dilated thou mayest begin to run in the way of My commandments. And then thou shalt say that *the sufferings of this time are not worthy to be compared with the glory to come, that shall be revealed in us* (Rom. viii, 18).

Bk. III, ch. li.

I do not know if you are still feeling as you did when you last wrote, but I am sending you in answer this passage from the Canticle of Canticles, which describes so vividly a soul in a state of dryness, who can find no comfort anywhere: *I went down into the garden of nuts to see the fruits of the valleys, and to look if the vineyard had flowered, and the pomegranates budded. I knew not: my soul troubled me for the chariots of Aminadab* (Cant. vi, 10, 11).

That is a picture of our souls. How often we go down to the fertile valleys where we found spiritual food, to the pleasant fields of Scripture where we discovered so many treasures, but which now seem like a waterless desert. We no longer know where we are: instead of peace and light our lot is darkness and distress, but like the Bride we know the cause of this trial. We are not yet in our fatherland, but have still to be tried by temptation as gold in the furnace. Sometimes we feel utterly abandoned, and cannot make sure whether the *chariots*, that is, the noise and commotion which surround us, are within or without.

We do not know, but Jesus knows, and He sees our sorrow, and suddenly in the dark night, His voice is heard: *Return, return, O Sulamitess: return, return that we may behold thee* (ibid., vi, 12).

L.

DECEMBER 20

If I should know all things that are in the world, and should not be in charity, what help would it be to me in the sight of God, who will judge me by my deeds?

Bk. I, ch. ii.

He is truly great, who is great in charity.

Ibid., ch. iii.

Sœur Geneviève asked her for a farewell word: "I have said all that there is to say . . . the work is done . . . only love counts."

N.V.

DECEMBER 21

What can I do for my sins but humbly confess them and lament them, and incessantly implore Thy mercy for them? Hear me, I beseech Thee, in Thy mercy, when I stand before Thee, O my God.

All my sins displease me exceedingly; I will never commit them any more; I am sorry for them, and will be sorry for them as long as I live: I am willing to do penance for them, and to make satisfaction to the utmost of my power. Forgive, O my God, forgive me my sins, for Thy holy Name's sake. Save my soul, which Thou hast redeemed with Thy precious blood.

Bk. IV, ch. ix.

One morning during her last illness, when the Community were reciting the Confiteor at her bedside before she received Holy Communion, she was deeply affected by the sense of her own unworthiness, and confided later to Mère Agnès de Jésus: "When I saw Our Lord about to give Himself to me, I realized the urgent need for this humiliation: *I confess to Almighty God, to Blessed Mary ever a Virgin, to all the Saints, that I have sinned exceedingly.* . . How necessary at that moment to ask pardon of God! I felt like the publican, like the greatest of sinners, and was so moved at the thought of the whole court of Heaven imploring the Divine Mercy on my behalf."

She had copied on one of her breviary markers the following texts from the Gospel: *Lord, thou knowest that I love thee* (John xxi, 16); *be merciful to me a sinner* (Luke xviii, 13).

E.

DECEMBER 22

When thou shalt arrive thus far, that tribulation

becomes sweet and savoury to thee for the love of
Christ; then think that it is well with thee, for thou
hast found a paradise upon earth.

Bk. II, ch. xii.

> Pain, lifted up to Thee,
>   Is Pain no more:
> Joy casts aside the weeds
>   That Sorrow wore.

P.

DECEMBER 23

Oh, how great and honourable is the office of priests,
to whom it is given to consecrate with sacred words the
Lord of Majesty; to bless Him with their lips, to hold
Him with their hands, to receive Him with their own
mouth, and to administer Him to others!

Oh, how clean ought those hands to be, how pure that
mouth, how holy that body, how unspotted the heart of
a priest, into whom the Author of purity so often enters!

Bk. IV, ch. xi.

How great is our vocation! It is for Carmel to
preserve the salt of the earth. We offer our prayers and
sacrifices for the apostles of the Lord; whilst they
labour by word and example to win the souls of our
brethren, we must be their apostles.

H.

DECEMBER 24

(Christ.) I am the Lover of purity, and the Giver of
all holiness. I seek a pure heart, and there is the place
of My rest. Make ready for Me a large supper room,
and I will make the pasch with thee (Mark xiv, 15).

If Thou wilt have Me come to thee, and remain with
thee, purge out the old leaven, and make clean the

habitation of thy heart; for every lover prepareth the best and fairest room for his dearly beloved; and hereby is known the affection of him that entertaineth his beloved.

Bk. IV, ch. xii.

God, the divine Guest of our hearts, knows our poverty; all He asks, and expects to find, is an empty tabernacle.

L.

DECEMBER 25

May it please Thee, O Lord, to deliver me: for, poor wretch that I am, what can I do, and whither shall I go without Thee? How much the more difficult this is to me, so much the easier to Thee, is *this change of the right hand of the Most High* (Ps. lxxvi, ii).

Bk. III, ch. xxix.

In spite of all the graces Heaven was showering upon me, I was far from deserving them. I had a great desire for virtue, but all that I did was full of imperfections. I was so sensitive that I was a very great trial to others; it was useless to reason with me, for I was powerless to correct this fault. How could I expect to be received at Carmel? It would need a miracle to make me grow up once and for all, and God worked this little miracle on a date I shall never forget: December 25, 1886. The newborn Child turned my darkness into light; having for my sake become small and weak, He made me strong and brave; He armed me with His own weapons, and after that I *ran my course like a giant* (Ps. xviii), going from victory to victory. The fountain of my tears was dried up, and very rarely flowed again.

This is how I received the grace of conversion. They still treated me at home like a baby, filling my shoes with presents and putting them by the fire-place on Christmas Eve. My father had always shared in my delight as I drew out each gift, but this year Our Lord wished to cure me of my childishness. As I went up to my room after midnight Mass, I heard my father say: "Thérèse is too big a girl for such nonsense; I hope this will be the last year." The words cut me to the heart, and Céline, knowing my sensitiveness, begged me not to go down at once, as I would be sure to cry; but I was no longer the same, Jesus had changed my heart. I went down to the dining-room as though nothing had happened, and gaily pulled out the presents one by one, my father joining in the merriment. Céline thought that she was dreaming, but the fact remained that I had found once more the fortitude I had lost at the age of four and a half.

On that blessed night the third period of my life opened, the most beautiful and full of graces. The work I had attempted for years, was done in an instant by Our Lord, who accepted my good will. Like the Apostles, I could say: *Master, we have laboured all the night, and have taken nothing* (Luke v, 5), but Our Lord did more for me than He did for them, for He cast the net Himself and drew it in full of fish, and changed me into a fisher of souls. Charity took possession of my soul and filled me with the spirit of self-forgetfulness, and from that time I was always happy.

H.

DECEMBER 26

Whosoever loveth, knoweth the cry of this voice. A loud cry in the ears of God is the ardent affection of the soul, which saith: O my God, my love, Thou art all mine, and I am all Thine! Give increase to my love, that I may learn to taste with the interior mouth of the heart how sweet it is to love, and to swim, and to be dissolved in love.

Bk. III, ch. v.

I experienced several transports of love; one, during my novitiate, lasted a whole week, during which time I seemed to make use of a borrowed body, and felt far away from this world, which was veiled from my sight. Yet I was not burned by a real flame, and could enjoy these delights without hope of their breaking my hold upon life; whereas if the other experience (see March 29) of which I told you, had been prolonged for a few instants, I would have died ... Alas! I came back to earth, and immediately my soul become a prey once more to dryness of spirit.

H.

DECEMBER 27

The way of man is not always in his own power; but it belongs to God to give and to comfort when He will, and as much as He will, and to whom He will, and as it shall please Him, and no more.

Some, wanting discretion, have ruined themselves upon occasion of the grace of devotion: because they were desirous of doing more than they could, not weighing well the measure of their own weakness, but following rather the inclination of the heart than the dictates of reason. And because they presumptuously undertook greater things than were pleasing to God, there they quickly lost His grace.

They became needy, and were left in a wretched condition, who had built themselves a nest in heaven, to the end that being thus humbled and impoverished, they might learn not to trust to their own wings, but to hide themselves under Mine.

Bk. III, ch. vii.

O divine Sun! I am happy to feel so small and weak in Thy presence, and my heart is at peace. I know that all the eagles of Heaven take pity on me and protect me from the vultures—the fallen angels—whom I do not fear, as I am not destined to become their prey, but that of the divine Eagle.

O Word of God, my Saviour! as an Eagle Thou didst come down upon this land of exile, there to suffer and die, that Thou mightest carry up with Thee the souls of men into the very bosom of Love, the Blessed Trinity.

The Saints have done great things for Thee in the folly of their love, for they were eagles, but I am too little to attempt great things, and my folly is the hope that I shall become the victim of Thy love; my folly is to count on the intercession of the Angels and Saints that I may fly up to Thee with Thine own wings. . . I cherish the hope that one day Thou wilt swoop down upon me and carry me up until I am lost, a willing victim, in the fiery heart of the furnace of Love.

H.

DECEMBER 28

Many examine who is greatest in the kingdom of God, who know not if they shall be worthy to be numbered among the least. It is a great matter to be even the least in heaven, where all are great; because all shall be called, and shall be the children of God. The least shall be as a thousand, and the sinner of a hundred years shall die.

For when the disciples asked *who was the greater in the kingdom of heaven?* they received this answer:

Unless you be converted, and become as little children, you shall not enter into the kingdom of heaven. Whosoever therefore shall humble himself as this little child, he is the greater in the kingdom of heaven (Matt. xviii, 1, 3, 4).

Bk. III, ch. lviii.

Speaking of the Communion of Saints, she said: "With the virgins we shall be virgins, with the doctors we shall be doctors, with the martyrs we shall be martyrs, for all the Saints are our kindred; but those who followed the way of spiritual childhood will always keep the charm of children.

From my earliest years God has given me the conviction that I would die young."

N.V.

DECEMBER 29

Neither desire to be singularly praised or beloved: for this belongs to God alone, who hath none like to Himself. Neither desire that anyone's heart should be set on thee; nor do thou let thyself be taken up with the love of anyone; but let Jesus be in thee and in every good man.

Bk. II, ch. viii.

My love for them (the novices) is so disinterested that I do not even want them to know of it, but I would be ready to give my life for them. By the grace of God I have never tried to win their affection. I knew that my mission was to lead them to God and to you, dear Mother, who represent God to them, and whom they are therefore bound to love and respect.

H.

DECEMBER 30

Keep thyself with Jesus both in life and death, and commit thyself to His care who alone can help thee, when all others fail.

Bk. II, ch. vii.

Love watches, and sleeping, slumbers not: but like a lively flame, and a torch all on fire, it mounts upwards, and securely passes through all opposition.

Bk. III, ch. x.

A few nights before her death Sœur Geneviève came into the infirmary, and found her with eyes raised to Heaven and hands joined in prayer: "What are you doing? You ought to be trying to sleep."

"I cannot, so I am praying."

"What do you say to Our Lord?"

"Nothing; I am just loving Him."

Sum.

DECEMBER 31

Be pure and free interiorly, without being entangled by any creature. Thou must be naked and carry a pure heart to God, if thou wilt attend at leisure, and see how sweet the Lord is.

And indeed thou wilt never attain to this, unless thou be prevented and drawn by His grace; that so thou mayest all alone be united to Him alone, having cast out and dismissed all others.

Bk. II, ch. viii.

One morning after Holy Communion, Our Lord made me understand these words of the Canticle of Canticles: *Draw me: we will run after thee in the odour of thy ointments* (Cant. i, 3). When I pray: *draw me*, it is not necessary to add *and draw all those I love*. When a soul is led on by the sweet odour of Thy ointments, she does not run alone; the souls she loves are inevitably drawn after her. As a torrent carries down to the sea what lies in its path, so does the soul take with her all that she treasures when she casts herself into the boundless ocean of Thy love. Thou knowest, Lord, that my treasures are the souls Thou hast entrusted to me, and to whom my soul is closely knit.

I know not when my exile is to end, I may yet sing many times my evening hymn in praise of Thy tender mercies; but when my last day draws to its close, may I be allowed to make my own Thy words on the last evening of Thy mortal life: *I have glorified thee on the earth, I have finished the work which thou gavest me to do, I have manifested thy name to those whom thou hast given me, thine they were, and to me thou gavest them. Now they have known that all things which thou hast given me, are from thee: because the words which thou gavest me, I have given to them, and they have received them, and have believed that thou didst send me* (John xvii).

H.